Published by Tuttle Publishing, an imprint of Periplus Editions (HK) Ltd., with editorial offices at 364 Innovation Drive, North Clarendon, Vermont 05759 U.S.A. and 61 Tai Seng Avenue, #02-12, Singapore 534167

Copyright © 2009 Periplus Editions (HK) Ltd.

Library of Congress Control Number: 2009923718

ISBN 978-0-8048-4040-8

12 11 10 09   5 4 3 2 1

Printed in Singapore

Distributed by

North America, Latin America & Europe
Tuttle Publishing, 364 Innovation Drive
North Clarendon, VT 05759-9436 U.S.A.
Tel: 1 (802) 773-8930; Fax: 1 (802) 773-6993
info@tuttlepublishing.com
www.tuttlepublishing.com

Asia Pacific
Berkeley Books Pte. Ltd.
61 Tai Seng Avenue #02-12, Singapore 534167
Tel: (65) 6280-1330; Fax: (65) 6280-6290
inquiries@periplus.com.sg
www.periplus.com

Japan
Tuttle Publishing
Yaekari Building, 3rd Floor, 5-4-12 Osaki
Shinagawa-ku, Tokyo 141 0032
Tel: (81) 03 5437-0171; Fax: (81) 03 5437-0755
tuttle-sales@gol.com

TUTTLE PUBLISHING® is a registered trademark of Tuttle Publishing, a division of Periplus Editions (HK) Ltd.

Asian Cocktails

CREATIVE DRINKS INSPIRED BY THE EAST

HOLLY JENNINGS AND
CHRISTINE LEBLOND

PHOTOGRAPHY BY GORTA YUUKI
STYLING BY CHINATSU KAMBAYASHI

TUTTLE PUBLISHING
Tokyo · Rutland, Vermont · Singapore

Contents

Raising the bar

If you walked into a bar and asked for an Asian cocktail you'd probably get a blank stare from the bartender. It's about as vague a request as asking for an "American" cocktail. But if you mention a classic by name—like the Singapore Sling—or mention that you'd like a cocktail that uses Asian ingredients, such as ginger or lychees, you're likely to get a nod of recognition.

Asian cocktails are both old and new: they are classic, the familiar exotic and the newest taste sensation. In this collection of recipes you'll find cocktails such as the Japanese Cocktail, Bamboo Cocktail and Singapore Sling that date to the Golden Age of Cocktails (1860s to 1900) and to the Roaring Twenties. Some tropical rum-based classics, such as the Mai Tai and Scorpion, concocted sometime around the mid-twentieth century, are also included. (Since they've also made their way onto menus of Japanese steak houses and Chinese-American restaurants, how could we not include these Tiki Bar favorites?) These delicious oldies have names that evoke Asia and some were even created in Asia, but most don't have a single Asian ingredient in them.

It's taken a new generation of mixologists, many working behind bars in Asian restaurants or restaurants that feature Asian ingredients, to create cocktails that are

Drink less, but better . . . drink less, but enjoy to the fullest. —Stanislav Vadrna

more genuinely Asian than the exotic sounding drinks of yesteryear. The increased interest in Asian cuisines in the West has spilled over from the kitchen to the bar, where cocktails are often created to pair with the food being served. As a result some of the most interesting Asian cocktails are now being created in restaurant bars where the relationship between the bartender (bar "chef") and kitchen chef is symbiotic, and where the bartender has ready access to lots of fresh and dried Asian ingredients—from spices to fruits and herbs. The majority of the cocktails in *Asian Cocktails*, some created especially for this book, are examples of the new Asian cocktail.

Whether putting an Asian spin on a classic cocktail, such as the Jujube Manhattan, or creating a new drink altogether, there are a variety of ways that mixologists make a cocktail Asian. Some use Asian wines or liquors, such as sake, plum wine, shochu or Japanese whiskey while others infuse a Western liquor, usually vodka, with an Asian ingredient and use that as the basis for a unique cocktail. Others may use Asian mixers or other flavoring components, such as mango juice, Calpico, lychees, fresh Thai basil, fresh lemongrass, chiles or fresh ginger with Western or Asian wines or liquors.

As when making any cocktail, using good quality liquor and fresh ingredients is key. The balance of sweet and sour in relation to the liquor is the typical driver of flavor, though other flavors, like bitter (via "bitters") and spicy or piquant flavors, can add magic to the balance. Bitters are the umami of the bar—used in the same way a cook may use a small amount of fish sauce or anchovies to add nuance that's hard to pinpoint but noticeably lacking when absent. Just a couple of drops of these potent flavoring agents are used to give depth and interest to cocktails. Bitters also add a counterpoint to liqueurs, fruits, syrups or other sweet ingredients, sometimes working along with sour citrus to do this. As the interest in well-crafted and vintage cocktails rises, old brands/recipes of bitters are being resurrected and new ones are being created. Orange bitters, which is used periodically in this book, is infused with orange peel and spices. Aromatic bitters, such as Angostura, tend to be bolder and more complex, with greater amounts of cinnamon, clove and anise.

Whereas bitters have long been used in the West in cocktails, spice is a relatively new phenomenon introduced via Asian cocktails, where spicy ginger or chiles add a noticeable kick to drinks—adjusted, of course, to personal taste. And while salt, the last of the five basic taste sensations, is not normally included in cocktails, except to rim a margarita, it is used to heighten flavor in the distinctive Silk Road, Nashi Cocktail and Little Tokyo Cooler—much in the way a pinch of salt is used in baking.

HOW TO USE THIS BOOK

If Asian cocktails haven't found their way into your neighborhood bar/restaurant bar, you can easily make them at home using the recipes in this book—once you stock your bar and pantry with some basic equipment and ingredients. The sections at the beginning of the book— "Glassware," "Stocking the Bar," and "Tools and Techniques"—will help you set up a basic bar and teach you the techniques you'll need to craft a cocktail. The recipes in "Syrups and Infused Spirits" are the jumping-off point for many great cocktails. When making cocktails using infused spirits remember to plan ahead as most infusions take an average of two or three days, and some longer, to make. Syrups can be prepared very quickly— they only need sufficient time to cool before using.

While the focus of this book is on the use of fresh ingredients, there are a variety of new flavored vodkas and liqueurs on the market with Asian flavors: Pama (pomegranate), Zen (green tea), SoHo (lychee), Hangar One vodka (kaffir lime), to name a few. We've included a handful of drinks that use some of these high-quality products as they need only be shaken or stirred with one or two other ingredients to create a cocktail. This is worth considering when you are entertaining and need to make several drinks quickly.

The final chapter includes nonalcoholic drinks and bar snacks, which provide good options for satisfying every taste and level of hunger when entertaining. The resource guide will help you track down hard-to-find ingredients and the index will help you to cross-reference specific ingredients to maximize their use while they're fresh.

Most of all we hope you have fun using this book and introducing your friends to the great flavor of Asian cocktails—both classic and new.

Tools & Techniques

The tools listed below will enable you to make any cocktail in this book—and scores beyond. Equal in importance to having the right tools is understanding the basic techniques used to make a cocktail—muddling, shaking and so on. In addition to these techniques, here is a key rule of thumb to remember: do not become impatient when stirring or shaking a cocktail. A properly chilled cocktail, and thereby properly diluted, will consist of 25 percent water, which serves to soften liquor's hard edges. So always shake or stir for the full amount of recommended time. Your guests will appreciate the result even when they have to wait another ten or fifteen seconds!

BOSTON SHAKER This two-part shaker is comprised of two tumblers: one metal and one glass (a.k.a. pint glass or mixing glass). A bar strainer is required to use this shaker. This is the choice of professional bartenders because the glass portion allows for visual checks, which is especially important when muddling, it's easy to clean and the seal is superior.

MIXING GLASS This heavy bottomed 16-ounce (500-ml) glass is used for cocktails that are stirred, and some are even spouted for easy pouring. It is used for muddling and, when not spouted, is the ideal receptacle for constructing cocktails that are meant to be shaken (because the clear mixing glass allows you to see what you're doing). The glass receptacle of a Boston shaker can serve as a mixing glass.

COCKTAIL SHAKER Sometimes called a "martini shaker" or "cobbler shaker," these three-part shakers are usually comprised of a metal tumbler, a lid with a built-in strainer and a cap. They come in all kinds of wonderful designs and, with their gleaming stainless steel surface and rounded Art Deco lines, evoke machine-

age glamour. Though they're easier to master than the Boston shaker, their seal generally isn't as effective. If you do not own a mixing glass, the base of the cocktail shaker can be used for muddling ingredients and stirring cocktails.

BAR STRAINERS There are two main types

of bar strainers—the Hawthorne and the julep—with the Hawthorne being more common. The Hawthorne strainer (top, left) is designed to be used with a metal tumbler.The Hawthorne strainer has a built-in spring to help hold it snugly in place and to help strain ice. It can be used with a mixing glass, though it doesn't fit as well (its built-in spring will constantly try to pop out of the narrower mouth). Look for a Hawthorne strainer that has either two or four prongs (four is better) sticking out from the edge of the strainer. The julep strainer (bottom, left) is designed to be used with a mixing glass. Its design is much simpler than the Hawthorne: it consists of a concave bowl perforated with small holes. We like to use the julep strainer when fruit or herbs have been muddled in a cocktail. Bits of fruit pulp and herbs can get stuck in the spring in the Hawthorne strainer, which makes for longer clean-up time.

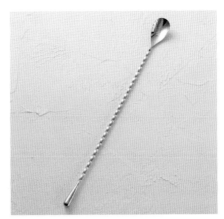

BAR SPOON This long stainless steel spoon is used to stir cocktails and layer fancy drinks like the pousse-café (don't worry, none of the recipes in this book require such sleight of hand). Its length allows it to reach to the bottom of a mixing glass or the tallest Collins glass. It can also be used for measuring (the spoon holds about 1 teaspoon). Its twisted swizzle stick–like handle is designed to help with stirring.

JIGGER This is essential for the home bar. The dual-sided and cone-shaped metal jigger measures a larger amount on one side and a smaller amount on the other side—traditionally 1 1/2 ounces (45 ml), or a "jigger," and 3/4 ounce (22 ml), or a "pony." Today jiggers come in many different sizes.

MUDDLER A pestle made of wood, metal or plastic that varies in length from about 8 to 12 inches (20 to 30 cm). The flattened end is used to crush ingredients and thereby release juice, oils and flavor.

MISCELLANEOUS TOOLS
Paring knife and chef's knife
Cutting board
Blender and/or small food processor
Can opener
Corkscrew
Measuring spoons
Small fine-meshed kitchen strainer
Citrus juicer
Fine grater (optional)

MUDDLING This technique is used to extract and combine flavors. Sometimes ingredients are muddled with sugar, which acts as an abrasive and helps to extract flavor. Ingredients are placed in the bottom of a mixing or serving glass or a cocktail shaker and are firmly pressed with the flat end of the muddler until all of the juices are extracted and the sugar is dissolved. Herbs will become transparent when sufficiently muddled.

STIRRING Stirring combines and chills cocktail ingredients, though not as rapidly as shaking. Cocktails that do not contain juice, dairy or eggs should be stirred for the best presentation. (Shaking can make some liquors cloudy and leave shards of ice in the glass. Cocktails like a Martini or Manhattan are meant to be perfectly clear.) To stir a cocktail, add the ingredients to a mixing glass or the base of a cocktail shaker. Add ice and stir for 20 to

tools & techniques

30 seconds, ideally using a bar spoon. To stir with a bar spoon twirl the spoon back and forth between your fingers while moving the spoon up and down—you are actually churning the cocktail! The handle is twisted, making it easy to twirl it between your fingers.

SHAKING Cocktails that contain juice, dairy or egg should be shaken. Sometimes cocktails containing heavier fruit-based liqueurs are also shaken.

To make a cocktail using a Boston shaker, add the ingredients and ice to the mixing glass. Place the metal tumbler over the top of the mixing glass and give the metal tumbler a firm slap to secure the two together. (Don't apply brute force or you may create a stubborn seal that's very hard to dislodge.) To test the seal, holding the top of the metal tumbler, carefully pick up the Boston shaker (about $\frac{1}{2}$ inch/1.25 cm) off the counter. Holding the shaker with both hands, and keeping the metal tumbler below the glass, shake vigorously for a full 10 to 15 seconds. (Note: cocktails with eggs should be shaken with extra enthusiasm to emulsify the egg).

To dislodge the shaker, place the shaker on a counter metal side down (for safety reasons, it's important that the metal part is on the bottom). With the heel or side of your palm (a loose fist can be formed if that is more comfortable), firmly tap the metal tumbler just below the rim, right about at the point where the glass comes into contact with it. Note that almost always, the glass will be "leaning" to one side or the other. You want to tap it on the side that the glass is leaning into, and this will almost always allow you to open the shaker with just a single tap. You may have to whack the side of the shaker a couple of times to release the seal, especially if you're just getting the knack of it.

To make a cocktail using a cocktail shaker, simply remove the lid, add the ingredients and ice, replace the lid with the cap snugly in place, and shake vigorously for 10 to 15 seconds. To strain the cocktail, remove just the cap.

BUILDING This is the simplest of all cocktail making techniques. To build a drink, a highball glass is filled with ice, the ingredients are added, stirred a few times, garnished (if applicable), and served. It doesn't get any easier.

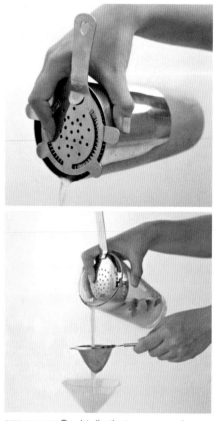

STRAINING Cocktails that are served up, like a Martini, are always strained and some cocktails that are served over ice are strained, particularly when it's not desirable for muddled ingredients to end up in the serving glass. The Hawthorne strainer, as shown in the top photograph, rests across top of the metal tumbler; its prongs allow it to sit firmly on the lip of the metal tumbler.

The julep strainer is placed into a mixing glass and held at an angle (concave side inward toward the ice) to hold back ice as the cocktail is poured (as shown in the bottom, left photograph). Periodically, some cocktails are double strained. To double strain a cocktail, using a typical bar strainer, pour the cocktail through a small fine-mesh kitchen strainer into the serving glass. (See the photograph bottom, left).

MAKING GARNISHES Classic garnishes are timeless but you can also have fun and create your own. In fact, the Asian twist on many drinks in this book are revealed in the garnishes—whether it be a speared lychee, a piece of candied ginger or a stem of fresh Thai basil inserted in a glass. Here is a description of some basic garnishes used in this book. **TO MAKE LEMON AND LIME WEDGES,** first trim off both ends with a paring knife. If you're working with a lime, cut it in half crosswise; if a lemon, cut it in half lengthwise. Cut each half into equal-size wedges. **TO MAKE LEMON, LIME, YUZU OR CALAMANSI TWISTS,** cut off one end of the fruit. Set the cut end down on a cutting board and, using a paring knife, cut strips of zest from the top of the fruit to the bottom, following the curve of the fruit. There should be a small amount of inner white pith on the twist to provide some sturdiness. **IF MAKING ORANGE TWISTS,** cut both ends off the fruit, and cut twists from the middle of the orange downward, turning the orange over and

repeating when one side is completed. Before adding a twist to a cocktail, squeeze to help release the aromatic oils. **TO MAKE FRUIT WHEELS,** cut off both ends of the fruit, cutting in deep enough to get past the pith and reveal the fruit. Cut the fruit into $1/4$-inch (6-mm) round slices, or wheels. To allow the wheel to be hung from the rim of a glass, cut the wheel through the peel up to its center. **TO MAKE HALF-WHEELS,** cut the whole wheels in half and then make a slit from the center of the slice up to the white pith.

TO RIM A GLASS To apply a rimmer to a glass, place the dry rimmer ingredients in a shallow saucer. The next step is to moisten the outside edge of the glass with a sticky substance so that the dry ingredients will stick to it. You can do this in one of two ways. If citrus is used in the cocktail, cut a slit in a wedge of the same type of citrus used in the cocktail. Sit the wedge on the rim of the glass and slide it around the perimeter, squeezing the wedge slightly. If the cocktail doesn't use citrus, pour one of the sugary ingredients used in the drink, such as triple sec or a liqueur, in a flat saucer. If the cocktail doesn't contain a sugary ingredient, which is unlikely, pour some 2:1 simple syrup in a saucer. To moisten the rim, dip the glass into the saucer with the

sugary liquid. To rim the glass, hold the glass by its base at a 45-degree angle and allow the rim to rest on the dry ingredients, rotating the glass until the whole rim is coated. Do not dip the moistened glass face down into the dry ingredients as this will cause the rimmer to be on the inside and outside of the glass—which is something you absolutely do not want. (Is salt an ingredient IN a margarita? I think not!)

> **TIP: Fruit should be juiced or muddled at room temperature because chilled fruit will yield only about half as much juice. If you forget to remove fruit from the refrigerator before the cocktail hour, run warm water over the fruit. To increase the juice extracted from citrus, on a counter, firmly press on the citrus fruit with the heel of your palm and roll back and forth.**

Glassware

Serving a cocktail in the glass it's meant for increases the enjoyment of a drink—but all you really need are a few basic types, many of which you probably already have on hand. To simplify things, we've highlighted only those that are required for the recipes in this book—there are several more specialized glasses available.

HIGHBALL GLASS (8–10 OZ/250–300 ML)
This medium-tall glass is used for simple built drinks called highballs—often using just two ingredients.

COLLINS GLASS (10–12 OZ/300–350 ML)
Named after the collins cocktail, this glass is a taller, more elegant version of the highball glass. It is often larger than the highball glass.

ROCKS GLASS (6–10 OZ/175–300 ML)
Sometimes called an old-fashioned glass after the famous cocktail, this squat tumbler is intended for drinks served over ice—or on the "rocks."

COCKTAIL GLASS (4–8 OZ/125–250 ML)
This is also called a martini glass, after the cocktail of that name. It is used for all shaken or stirred drinks that are served up—that is, not over ice. All cocktail glasses are stemmed and have a conical bowl, though traditionally those that have gently rounded sides are referred to as cocktail glasses and those with straight sides as martini glasses. Either style can be used. We prefer 6-ounce (175-ml) or smaller cocktail glasses because very large cocktails do not remain properly chilled.

CHAMPAGNE FLUTE (6–8 OZ/175–250 ML)
The narrow mouth on this glass is designed to keep many bubbles from escaping too quickly. The older style widemouthed champagne saucer is virtually never used anymore for this reason.

RED AND/OR WHITE WINE GLASS (8–12 OZ/250–350 ML)
Red wine glasses are slightly larger than white wine glasses and have a slightly more bulbous shape. The Sake Sangria is served in wine glasses—and though white is preferred—either will do.

PINT GLASS (16 OZ/475 ML)
This is equivalent to the mixing glass used for preparing cocktails. The Imperial pint glass is 20 ounces (600 ml), however, we use the American 16-ounce (475-ml) glass for the cocktails in this book. It is primarily used to serve beer, but we use it to serve large cocktails.

PILSNER GLASS (10–14 OZ/300–400 ML)
This tall glass tapers from the mouth to the base. It is typically footed and is primarily used to serve beer, however, we use it to serve tall cocktails.

> **TIP: For the best presentation and drinking satisfaction, glasses used for cocktails that are served up rather than on the rocks should always be chilled.**

Glasses from left to right: pint glass, rocks glass, collins glass, champagne flute, cocktail glasses (two variations), rocks glass, pilsner, nontraditional rocks glass

Stocking your bar

Having a well-stocked bar is one of the luxuries of good living, and the sign of a generous host. This is a complete list of supplies needed to make every cocktail in this book, including some substitutions (check the recipes to learn which are meant as substitutions). Ingredients are organized in descending order by the most frequently used within each category.

SPIRITS
Vodka (unflavored, citrus or citron and orange); **Gin; Rum** (light, dark, aged,151, coconut-flavored rum); **Tequila** (silver, reposado and añejo); **Brandy; Fruit brandy** (apricot); **Bourbon; Rye whiskey** (substitute bourbon); **Single-malt scotch; Shochu/Soju; Wokka Saki**

WINE/SAKE
Sparkling wine (such as champagne, cava and prosecco); **White wine, fruity** (such as Reisling); **Sake; Japanese plum wine**

FORTIFIED WINE/APERATIFS
Vermouth, sweet and dry (Sweet vermouth refers to red vermouth, the best of which is traditionally from Italy. Dry vermouth is white, and the best is traditionally from France.); **Lillet Blanc** (a French aperitif fortified with brandy); **Sherry, medium dry** (a Spanish wine fortified with brandy); **Pimm's No. 1 Cup** (a British aperitif fortified with gin); **Campari** (This extremely bitter aperitif is sometimes classified as bitters and sometimes as a spirit due to its high 20 percent alcoholic content.)

LIQUEURS
Triple sec/Cointreau (Triple sec is a generic term for orange liqueur, some of which are quite sweet and low in alcohol. Cointreau is a drier, more sophisticated orange liqueur. It's handy to have both, though one can be substituted for the other if the amount used is adjusted or if the amount of simple syrup, if included in the cocktail, is adjusted.); **Schnapps** (peach and apple); **Crèmes** (noyeaux, peche [peach], mure, cassis); **Fruit** (black raspberry [such as Chambord], raspberry [such as Aqua Perfecta], black cherry [Cherry Heering], pear [such as Marie Brizard's Poire William or Mathilde Pear Liqueur], lychee [SoHo Litchi], pomegranate [Pama]); **Other** (green tea [Zen], amaretto, Bénédictine, Licor 43, anisette)

MIXERS
Juices, fresh and bottled; Club soda; Spicy ginger ale or "beer," such as Reed's or Blenheim; Teas; Calpico

Here is a basic citrus shopping guide:
1 lemon yields 1½ ounces (45 ml) juice
1 lime yields 1 ounce (30 ml) juice
1 tangerine yields 2½ ounces (75 ml) juice
1 orange yields 2½ to 3 ounces (75 to 90 ml) juice

SWEETENERS AND FLAVORING AGENTS
You can use homemade syrups for most of the recipes in this book, however, there are some instances when the syrup called for can't be easily replicated at home—such as cane or mango syrup. In those cases it will be easiest to purchase ready-made syrup. Angostura is easy to find in any grocery store. Orange bitters is available at specialty stores or online.
Syrups (simple, grenadine [homemade or store-bought], orgeat or almond, mango, rose, coconut, caramel, cane, blackberry); **Bitters** (Angostura and orange [Fee Brothers; Gary Regan's No. 6 (the latter is the more bitter of the two)]; **Sugars** (White, honey, demerara or raw sugar, brown sugar); **Sweetened lime juice** (calamansi or other such as Rose's or Stirrings's Clarified Key Lime); **Herbs, Spices and Aromatics**

GARNISHES
Maraschino cherries (for a more adult alternative to the bright-red artificially colored cherries that top ice cream Sundays, try Luxardo brand or make homemade maraschino cherries [search online for recipes]); **Citrus and other fruits** (for wedges, twists and fruit wheels); **Kosher or sea salt** for rimming; **Sugar** (white, demerara, raw or honey granules) for rimming; **Miscellaneous:** Crystallized ginger candy, pickled ginger, dried coconut shavings, fresh edible flowers, pineapple leaves

MISCELLANEOUS SUPPLIES
Ice, Cocktail picks, Miniature bamboo forks, Tiny Paper Umbrellas (for the Tiki Bar effect), **Straws, Eggs, Dark chocolate, Ice cream, Heavy cream, Cream of coconut**

Essential ingredients

Many Asian herbs, aromatics, spices, fruits and juices that were once considered exotic are now readily available through large supermarket chains, natural food stores, farmers markets and of course Asian markets and the Internet (see Resources, page 108). If your local grocery store doesn't carry something, ask for it. Sometimes that's all it takes.

Asian Pear Firm when ripe and exceedingly juicy, this subtle-tasting pear replaces pureed peaches in the Asian Pear Bellini (page 88). The season for Asian pears is late summer and early fall, extending the traditional height-of-summer Bellini season. Select the most fragrant pears with little or no brown spots. Asian pears should be stored in the refrigerator, where they will keep for several weeks. It is also called nashi pear, Japanese pear or Chinese pear.

Calamansi This small golf ball–shaped citrus from the Philippines has a very special flavor that's midway between a lime, a lemon and a tangerine. Fresh calamansi is hard to find in the United States so for our Calamansi Daiquiri (page 47) we use frozen calamansi juice, which is sometimes referred to as frozen pulp, and is sold in the frozen section of Asian markets that cater to a Filipino clientele. You might ask your local Asian market, food co-op or gourmet store to get you the fresh fruit or frozen juice or pulp if they don't already carry it. A second best substitute is presweetened calamansi concentrate. It is sometimes also spelled kalamansi.

Calpico This noncarbonated Japanese beverage comes in original and flavored and in either a ready-to-drink or a concentrate form. It has a light, milky and yogurtlike flavor. No wonder—it's made with water, nonfat milk and lactic acid.

The unflavored original Calpico is used for the cocktails in this book.

Cardamom This aromatic spice is native to southern India but grows in other tropical areas in Asia. Cardamom seeds are available ground or in pods. We use the pods, which are muddled in gin and rum cocktails to release the sweet-spicy flavor of the small seeds hiding inside. Any type of cardamom pod you can find will work, but if you have a choice, buy the green pods—they are the most fragrant.

Chiles We use the fiery heat of chiles to infuse simple syrups and liquors and muddle them fresh in cocktails. The most readily available Asian chiles in U.S. markets are the Thai chile (also known as the bird's-eye chile, bird chile, or Thai bird chile) and the finger chile (also known as the Dutch or Holland chile). The small Thai chile, measuring only about $1/2$ inches (3.75 cm) long and $1/8$ inch (3 mm) in diameter, packs a lot of heat. The Serrano chile, and secondarily the jalapeño pepper, can be substituted in like proportion for the finger chile, which is about 4 inches (10 cm) long and $1/2$ inch (1.25 cm) in diameter, or in double amount if replacing the much hotter Thai chile. Be careful when handling Thai chiles—hold then by the stem, avoid touching the seeds and don't rub your eyes!

Coconut Native to Malaysia, the coconut palm grows throughout the tropical world. Its seed, the coconut, is used to make a variety of products—oil, vinegar, juice, milk, cream and more. We use coconut-flavored rum, flaked coconut, presweetened cream of coconut and coconut syrup in five different cocktails.

Cucumber The fresh flavor of cucumber is a great addition to cocktails. The recipes in this book call for the burpless thin-skinned varieties of cucumber that are either seedless or have relatively few seeds. The best options are the mildly sweet Japanese cucumber, the baby or "mini" cucumber, the Armenian cucumber (which is actually a melon) or the English or "hot house" cucumber. If you use a particularly large English cucumber, you should remove the seeds. If you use the common garden-variety slicing cucumber, it should be peeled and deseeded.

Cumin Seeds This fragrant nutty-flavored seed is used in the Indian-inspired Cyclone (page 46) and in Curry Popcorn (page 103). Popular in Asian, Middle Eastern and Mediterranean cuisines, cumin seed is often toasted to heighten its flavor and aroma.

Five Spice Powder This Chinese spice blend usually consists of equal parts cinnamon, cloves, fennel seed, star anise and Szechuan peppercorns, though sometimes additional spices are added.

It's very flavorful so just a small amount is needed to add an Asian touch to cocktails. We use it to dust the Lychee Alexander (page 70) and as an ingredient in the rimmer for the Asian Pear Bellini (page 88).

Ginger The pungent bite of this aromatic root makes it one of the most popular ingredients in Asian cocktails, and the most adaptable. It can be used in very small amounts for a subtle effect or larger amounts to give an assertive gingery bite. We use the fresh root to infuse syrups and spirits and muddle directly in cocktails; candied ginger and sliver thin slices of fresh or pickled ginger as garnishes; and spicy ginger ale, or "beer," as a mixer or to top off cocktails. (Spicy ginger ale cannot be substituted with regular ginger ale.)

Ginger juice To juice ginger, place small pieces of peeled ginger in a sturdy garlic press and press to release the juice. Alternatively, you may finely grate the ginger, bundle it in a piece of cheesecloth and press with your fingers to release the juice. Japanese ginger graters do an excellent job of extracting juice, but they are a single-purpose gadget.

Herbs, Fresh To keep herbs fresh, rinse in several changes of very cold water to clean and revitalize them, then drain them. Place the herbs stem-side down in a glass of water, place a plastic bag over the top, secure the bag around the glass with a rubber band to keep as much air out as possible and place in the refrigerator. Change the water every couple of days. The herbs should last a week. If you find only shisho leaves rather than the shiso on the stalk, rinse the leaves under cold water, shake off excess moisture and store in the refrigerator in a plastic bag with a slightly dampened paper towel. The leaves will last only a few days.

Fresh Coriander (Cilantro) This pungent bright green herb is a staple of Asian and Mexican cooking. It is the plant of the coriander seed. It is also called Chinese parsley.

Mint Peppermint and spearmint are the two most popular varieties of this herb, which grows worldwide. Our brethren behind the bar have long muddled, infused and garnished with this versatile and refreshing herb to create classic cocktails such as the Whiskey Smash, the Mint Julep and the Mojito. This collection of recipes continues mint's traditional place behind the bar in rum-, whiskey and sake-based cocktails as well as a number of nonalcoholic drinks.

Shiso Part of the mint and basil family, this Japanese herb has a stimulating pinelike aroma and a distinct astringent flavor all its own—a combination of mint, cinnamon and clove with hints of cumin. Japanese red shiso is less common than the green variety and is typically used for

Ginger root
Five spice powder
Lemongrass
Yuzu
Cumin seeds
Passion fruit
Raw sugar
Shiso
Jujube
Jasmine tea
Mango juice
Chrysanthemum
Jasmine flowers
Pomegranate juice
Orange flower water
Rose water
Calpico

pickling. Shiso has a large rounded leaf with a jagged edge and pointed top. Look for green shiso in Asian markets specializing in Japanese produce. If you don't live near an Asian market, why not ask the manager of your local Japanese restaurant if you can buy some from them. (We've tried it; it works!) Other varieties of shisho exist in Vietnam and Korea. It is also called perilla or Japanese basil.

Thai Basil This wonderful variety of basil is increasingly available at grocery stores. It has a purple stem and purple flowers, dark green pointed leaves and a distinct aroma of anise. If you can't find Thai basil, you may substitute sweet Italian basil. It is also called anise or licorice basil.

Hibiscus Flowers, Dried This brightly colored tropical flower has an astringent cranberry-like flavor with citrus overtones. Dried hibiscus flowers are commonly used to make herbal tea. In *Asian Cocktails* we use dried hibiscus flowers, or "tea," to infuse vodka, which lends a lovely red color to The Hibiscus Petal (page 38). It is often mixed with more mild herbal or fruit flavors to create herbal signature blends. One hundred percent hibiscus tea is easy to find in natural food stores or can be ordered online.

Jasmine Flowers, Dried These aromatic flowers are used to make an herb tea called jasmine flower tea and to flavor green tea, and sometimes oolong tea, to create what is often simply called jasmine tea. We use the green tea–based jasmine tea to infuse vodka and brew it for use as a mixer.

Jujube Also known as Chinese red dates or simply "red dates," this sweet red-colored date has been cultivated in China

for more than 4,000 years. There is another variety of jujube that is slightly larger and brown or black in color, but it is less common. Fresh jujubes range in size from 1 to 2 inches (2.5 to 5 cm) in diameter; when dried, they shrink to $3/8$ to $3/4$ inch (1 to 2 cm) in diameter. We use a jarred Asian product called "jujube tea" in two whiskey-based cocktails. Jujube tea is a confusing label for Westerners because this product has the consistency of marmalade—thinly sliced jujubes are suspended in a thick sweet syrup. You can find jujube tea and dried jujubes at Asian markets, especially those selling Chinese and Korean products.

Lemongrass True to its name, this Southeast Asian herb has a wonderful lemony flavor and aroma that is derived from citral, an essential oil found in lemon peel. We puree it, make candied lemongrass straws with it—which serve double duty as a garnish and straw—and use it to infuse syrups, liquor and tea. Fresh lemongrass can be found at Asian markets and is increasingly available in mainstream grocery stores. When purchasing lemongrass look for firm greenish-white stalks with a smooth (not wrinkled) surface. Pick the thicker stalks, as these will be more flavorful. To store, place in a plastic bag or wrap in plastic wrap and place in the vegetable crisper drawer in your refrigerator, where it will keep for several weeks. Or you can freeze the stalks for up to 3 months. If your access to fresh lemongrass is sporadic, we suggest that you buy several stalks at a time and freeze them for later. To save room in your freezer, cut off the top one-third of the stalk and then freeze. To prepare for use, cut the very hard portion—about $1/2$ to 1 inch (1.25 to 2.5 cm)—off the bottom

of the stalk. Cut off the green woody top section (generally about the top one-third of the stalk). Peel away the outer two or three layers of dried tough stalk. The remaining portion is now ready for crushing, chopping and so on.

Lychee Prized in China for its natural sweetness and delicate flavor, this small cream-colored fruit—about 1 to 2 inches (2.5 to 5 cm) in diameter—is one of the most popular ingredients in Asian cocktails. Fresh lychees are covered with a red bumpy outer shell that is removed to reveal the fruit, which must then be deseeded. For convenience, we use canned pitted lychees, which are easy to find in Asian markets and increasingly in conventional grocery stores; lychee juice, which is easy to find in conventional grocery stores or natural food stores (Ceres brand is good quality and easy to find); and lychee liquor. It is sometimes spelled litchi or lichee.

Mango A native fruit of India, mangoes are produced in temperate climates around the world, including Florida and California. Mangoes come in different colors, so the best way to determine ripeness is to sniff the stem end—there should be a fruity fragrance when ripe—and to gently squeeze the fruit to detect a slight softness. We use mango juice, sometimes called mango nectar, for several rum or tequila-based cocktails, fresh mango for garnish and mango syrup.

Orange Blossom Water Also called orange flower water, this fragrant water is made from a distillation of bitter-orange blossoms. It is used to add a delicate and mysterious scent to the vodka-based Late Blossom (page 34).

Orgeat Syrup Pronounced "or-zat," not "or GEE at," this milky almond syrup is a signature ingredient in many classic cocktails, including the Mai Tai, Scorpion and Japanese Cocktail. It is well worth adding to your bar, though it can be hard to find in brick-and-mortar stores. However, if you don't mind paying shipping costs, it's easy to find online. Or you can search the web for recipes for making it at home. If you're making it at home, we suggest that you add some orange blossom water as this is what gives the syrup its unique character—but start with very small amounts and add gradually until you achieve just a hint of a floral bouquet. Easier-to-find almond syrup (not almond extract!) can be used as substitute, though it doesn't have the complexity of orgeat syrup.

Passion Fruit This tropical fruit has a wonderful sweet-tart flavor that's at home in cocktails. We use pulp from fresh fruit or bottled juice in vodka-, rum- and sake-based drinks, as well as the nonalcoholic Peach and Passion Fruit Smash (page 97). The variety of passion fruit that's easiest to find in the United States has dark purple skin. They are about 2 inches (5 cm) in length and are rounded or slightly egg-shaped. Pick fruit that has some weight to it, as this indicates more juice. Passion fruit is ripe when the skin is deeply wrinkled. To extract the pulp, cut the fruit in half crosswise and remove the pulp with a teaspoon. The pulp is filled with edible black seeds. If you wish to remove the seeds, force the pulp through a sieve with a rubber spatula, then discard the seeds. If you find bargain-priced passion fruit, buy lots and freeze the pulp and seeds together for use later.

Pomegranate Juice The singular pleasantly tart flavor and beautiful deep red color of pomegranates make them one of the world's most luxurious fruits. We use bottled fresh pomegranate juice to make homemade grenadine and Pomegranate-Ginger Syrup. Look for pomegranate juice in refrigerated coolers in your grocery store. Double check the label to make sure you're buying plain pomegranate juice—some are mixed with other fruits.

Rose Water This highly fragrant water—a distillation of rose petals—is used in very small amounts to flavor food or beverages. We use it to make rose syrup for the Lychee Rose Petal Martini (page 28).

Sugars Refined white sugar is great when what's needed is a neutral sweetener. But why not experiment with the world of possible sugar options? For a truly Asian simple syrup, why not make a simple syrup using palm sugar? In this book mixologists use demerara, raw sugar, whole cane sugar and syrup, vanilla sugar, honey and honey granules and more to add a distinct flavor to cocktails. Just remember that when using nonwhite sugar in cocktails the color will change, though this is only a "problem" if you deem it so, and the difference in color probably won't be apparent in cocktails made with amber-colored liquors.

Tamarind This slightly sweet but mostly sour flavoring agent, which is the pod of the tamarind tree, is used in Asian cuisines much as lemon is used in the west, though it is not acidic. Tamarind is available fresh in the pod, pressed into blocks of pulp and seeds or as a liquid concentrate. We use the liquid concen-

trate for its ready-to-use convenience. The consistency of the liquid concentrate may vary from brand to brand—ranging from a pastelike consistency to a pourable consistency of thinned ketchup. We used a concentrate with the consistency of the latter. If the concentrate you find has more of a pastelike consistency, use a little less tamarind than what is called for and dissolve it in a little warm water before combining it with other cocktail ingredients. You can find tamarind liquid concentrate in Asian markets, in natural foods stores with an international section and in some mainstream grocery stores.

Teas Whether infused in spirits or brewed for use as a mixer, a variety of straight and flavored teas—from green to spiced chai—are used to give a refreshing quality to Asian cocktails. When brewing tea for cocktails, use fresh loose-leaf tea for the best results. However, bagged tea can also be used. Different types of teas require different water temperature and steeping times. These are indicated in the recipes where teas are used.

Yuzu The juice and zest of this sour tangerine-size citrus are popular flavorings in Japanese cooking. It can be found fresh in Japanese markets and some gourmet shops during the winter months when it is in season. If you can find it, buy several fruit and freeze the juice for later use. We use bottled juice, which is much easier to find and available year-round. When buying bottled yuzu juice make sure you buy unsalted (unseasoned) juice. The bottled juice is expensive—but just a small amount is used per cocktail so a bottle will last a while. If don't have yuzu juice, substitute lemon juice.

essential ingredients

Syrups & Infused Spirits

Making homemade flavored syrups and infused spirits is creative and fun, and one of the easiest ways to create original and distinctive cocktails. You can use herbs, spices, aromatics and fruits to infuse syrups, vodka, gin and even rum—the only limit is really your own imagination. The basic infusion technique can be applied to any infusion, though some infusing times may vary.

   Here are some important tips for making home syrups and infusions. When straining flavored syrups or spirits use a fine-mesh sieve or a colander lined with cheesecloth. Press against the flavoring ingredients with a rubber spatula to extract as much flavor as possible. Flavored syrups should be stored in the refrigerator, where they will keep about three weeks. Infused spirits should last about one year. All spirits, infused or otherwise, should be tightly capped, placed out of direct sunlight, and should not be exposed to extreme heat or cold. When infusing vodka, avoid using potato- or rye-based vodkas as they are stronger flavored than other vodkas and compete with the flavor you're infusing. It's best to taste the infusion before straining and rebottling it to make sure the flavor is sufficiently strong. Remember to write the name of your homemade syrups and infusions on the bottles, and the date that you made them.

Thai Basil Syrup

Brown Sugar Syrup

Lemongrass and Kaffir Lime Leaf Syrup

Thai Chili Syrup

Rose Syrup

Shiso Syrup

SIMPLE SYRUP

Simple syrup is the most essential homemade ingredient for making cocktails. All recipes in the book use 1:1 simple syrup, or syrup made from equal parts sugar and water, unless otherwise noted.

Makes 1½ cups (375 ml)
1 cup (250 g) sugar
1 cup (250 ml) water

Combine the water and sugar in a small saucepan and bring to a boil over medium heat. Stir until the sugar dissolves then remove from the heat and cool. Store in a clean glass bottle or jar with a tight-fitting lid in the refrigerator.

VARIATION: 2:1 SIMPLE SYRUP To make a 2:1 simple syrup, follow the instructions above, but double the ratio of sugar to water—for example, 2 cups (500 g) sugar to 1 cup (250 ml) of water, which will yield 2 cups (500 ml) 2:1 syrup; or 1 cup (250 g) sugar to ½ cup (125 ml) of water, which will yield 1 cup (125 ml) 2:1 syrup.

BROWN SUGAR SYRUP

This 2:1 syrup adds a rich flavor and amber color to cocktails.

Makes 2 cups (500 ml)
1 cup (250 g) each light and dark brown sugar
1 cup (250 ml) water

Combine the water and the light and dark brown sugars in a small saucepan and bring to a boil over medium heat. Stir until the sugar dissolves then remove from the heat to cool. Store in a clean glass bottle or jar with a tight-fitting lid in the refrigerator.

GINGER SYRUP

This easily mixable and delicious syrup is one of our favorites.

Makes ½ cup (125 ml)
½ cup (125 ml) 2:1 Simple Syrup (see above)
One 2-in (5-cm) piece fresh ginger, peeled and sliced

Combine the 2:1 Simple Syrup and the sliced ginger in a small saucepan and bring to a boil. Reduce the heat and simmer for 5 minutes. Remove from the heat and steep for 30 minutes. Strain into a clean glass jar or bottle with a tight-fitting lid. Store in the refrigerator.

Citrus Syrup

Ginger Syrup

Lemongrass Syrup

Pomegranate-Ginger Syrup

ROSE SYRUP

In addition to being used in cocktails, rose syrup can be added to iced tea or drizzled over pastries and is delicious over vanilla ice cream. Red food coloring gives this syrup a pretty pink color reminiscent of roses. We prefer to use natural products whenever possible, but natural red food coloring is hard to track down. If you can find it, we recommend using it in place of conventional artificial coloring.

Makes 1¼ cups (300 ml)
1 cup (250 ml) 2:1 Simple Syrup (page 19)
1½ teaspoons strained freshly squeezed
   lemon juice
¼ cup (65 ml) rose water
1 to 2 drops of red food coloring

Place the 2:1 Simple Syrup in a small saucepan and bring to a gentle boil. Add the lemon juice and simmer, without stirring, for 10 minutes. Skim any foam that forms off the top. Add the rosewater and simmer 3 minutes more. Remove from the heat and set aside to cool. Add 1 drop of food coloring and stir. If the syrup isn't pink enough add another drop. Store in a clean glass bottle or jar with a tight-fitting lid in the refrigerator.

HONEY SYRUP

The delicately flavored syrup is a great addition to many cocktails.

Makes 1 cup (250 ml)
¼ cup (65 ml) Simple Syrup (page 19)
¾ cup (185 ml) honey

In a small saucepan over medium heat, add the Simple Syrup. When the Simple Syrup is near to the boiling point, add the honey. Stir until evenly combined. Remove from the heat and let cool. Store in a clean glass jar or bottle with a tight-fitting lid in the refrigerator.

LEMONGRASS SYRUP

This is one of the most popular syrups for Asian cocktails.

Makes 1½ cups (375 ml)
2 to 3 stalks fresh lemongrass
1½ cups (375 ml) Simple Syrup (page 19)

Wash the lemongrass and cut about ½ inch (1.25 cm) off the hard root ends and the top one-third off the stalks, and discard. Remove the tough outer layers and discard. Bruise the tender white stalks with the broad side of a chef's knife. Coarsely chop and set aside. Place the Simple Syrup in a small saucepan and bring to a gentle boil. Add the chopped lemongrass to the hot syrup, lower the heat and simmer for 20 minutes. Remove from the heat and set aside to cool completely. Strain into a clean glass jar or bottle with a tight-fitting lid. Store in the refrigerator.

VARIATION: Lemongrass and Kaffir Lime Leaf Syrup. This variation features the glossy dark-green kaffir lime leaf from the kaffir lime tree, which adds a wonderful exotic floral-citrus aroma. The leaves can be found at markets that sell Southeast Asian and Indian products or ordered online. To make Lemongrass and Kaffir Lime Leaf Syrup, prepare the Lemongrass Syrup as described, adding eight fresh or sixteen dried kaffir lime leaves or zest from 1 lime to the saucepan with the lemongrass and Simple Syrup. After the syrup has simmered and cooled, puree the mixture in a blender or food processor. Strain through a sieve and press on the solids to extract as much flavor as possible. Strain once more into a clean glass jar or bottle with a tight-fitting lid. Store in the refrigerator.

THAI BASIL SYRUP

This aromatic simple syrup with floral undertones pairs well with most Asian flavors.

Makes 1½ cups (375 ml)
1 cup (250 ml) water
1 cup (250 g) sugar
1 bunch Thai basil (about 1 oz/30 g)

In a saucepan, combine the water, sugar and basil (leaves and stems). Place over medium heat and stir frequently until the sugar has dissolved. When the syrup begins to simmer, remove from the heat. Let cool. Strain into a clean glass jar or bottle with a tight-fitting lid. Store in the refrigerator.

> VARIATION: Spicy Thai Basil Syrup. Follow the instructions for making Thai Basil Syrup, adding either one Thai chile or two small Serrano, finger or jalapeño chiles, cut into rings, to the saucepan with the water, sugar and basil.

CITRUS SYRUP

You can use these instructions to create any type of citrus simple syrup—from lime to lemon. Adjust the amount of citrus or simple syrup used according to the size of the citrus. To create a syrup with complexity, experiment with combinations of lime, lemon, blood orange, tangerine, Buddha's hand and/or Meyer lemon.

Makes ½ cup (125 ml)
½ cup (125 ml) Simple Syrup (page 19)
Zest and peel of 1 lemon

Combine the Simple Syrup and the zest and peel in a small saucepan and bring to a boil. Reduce the heat and simmer for 5 minutes. Remove from the heat and steep for 30 minutes. Strain into a clean glass jar or bottle with a tight-fitting lid. Store in the refrigerator.

THAI CHILI SYRUP

This syrup adds a spicy Asian kick to cocktails.

Makes 1 cup (250 ml)
1½ cups (375 ml) Simple Syrup (page 19)
1 Thai chile or 2 serrano or finger chiles, chopped (include seeds)

Place the Simple Syrup in a small saucepan and bring to gentle boil. Add the chopped chile and simmer for 15 minutes. Remove from the heat to let cool. Strain into a clean glass jar or bottle with a tight-fitting lid. Store in the refrigerator.

LYCHEE SYRUP

How many ways can the naturally sweet lychee be incorporated into cocktails? Let us count the ways: syrup, infused spirits, liqueur, freshly muddled fruit.

Makes 4 cups (1 liter)
One 20-ounce can of lychees (approx 15 lychees)
About 2 cups (500 ml) Simple Syrup (page 19)

Blend the lychees with their syrup. Place the blended lychees in a fine-meshed sieve and press with a spatula to extract as much juice as possible. Combine the strained blended lychees with equal parts Simple Syrup. Store in a clean glass jar or bottle with a tight-fitting lid in the refrigerator.

SHISO SYRUP

This highly distinctive and aromatic syrup gives cocktails a unique flavor that we love.

Makes 1½ cups (375 ml)
1 cup (250 ml) water
1 cup (250 g) sugar
30 to 35 shiso leaves (about 2 oz/60 g)

In a saucepan, combine the water, sugar and shiso. Place over medium heat and stir frequently until the sugar has dissolved. When the syrup begins to simmer, remove from the heat. Let cool. Strain into a clean glass jar or bottle with a tight-fitting lid. Store in the refrigerator.

POMEGRANATE-GINGER SYRUP

This naturally sweetened and slightly spicy syrup is the basis for an elegant champagne cocktail (page 79).

Makes 1 cup (250 ml)
3 cups (750 ml) pomegranate juice
½ cup (50 g) peeled and chopped fresh ginger

Combine the pomegranate juice and ginger in a saucepan and cook over medium heat until the liquid is reduced by two-thirds. Set aside to cool. Strain into a clean glass jar or bottle with a tight-fitting lid. Store in the refrigerator.

HOMEMADE GRENADINE

Now that fresh pomegranate juice is readily available, you can make home-made pomegranate syrup, or grenadine, that is free of artificial colors or flavoring. You can use it to make everything from a Shirley Temple to Pomegranate Royale (page 79).

Makes 1½ cups (375 ml)
1 cup (250 ml) fresh pomegranate juice, such as POM
1 cup (250 g) sugar

Combine the pomegranate juice and sugar in a small saucepan and bring to a boil over medium heat. Stir until the sugar dissolves then remove from the heat and cool. Store in a clean glass bottle or jar with a tight-fitting lid in the refrigerator.

BERRY-INFUSED GIN

This infused gin can be used in place of Saffron-infused Gin for the cocktail Fool's Gold (page 58).

4½ pints (900 g) blueberries or raspberries
One 750-ml bottle gin

Add the berries to the gin and set aside to infuse for 1½ weeks. Strain and rebottle.

LEMONGRASS-INFUSED VODKA OR GIN

This subtle infusion is a great base for Asian cocktails.

5 stalks fresh lemongrass
One 750-ml bottle vodka or gin

22

Wash the lemongrass and cut about ½ inch (1.25 cm) off the hard root ends and the top one-third off the stalks, and discard. Remove the tough outer layers and discard. Bruise the tender white stalks with the broad side of a chef's knife. Place the crushed stalks and the vodka or gin in a clean glass jar. Set aside at room temperature to infuse for 4 to 5 days. Taste. If the lemongrass flavor isn't strong enough, let rest for up to another 4 to 7 days, tasting periodically. Strain and rebottle the infused vodka or gin.

VARIATION: Peach and Lemongrass-Infused Vodka or Gin. We recommend you make this infusion in the summer with seasonal peaches. This infusion can be used in Fool's Gold (page 58) in place of Saffron-infused gin. To make this variation, prepare the infusion, as described above, adding 3 pounds (1.5 kg) of peaches that you've peeled, deseeded, and quartered to the jar with the alcohol and lemongrass. Set aside at room temperature to infuse for 1 week. Strain and rebottle the infused vodka or gin.

SAFFRON-INFUSED GIN

The yellow-orange stigmas of a crocus, saffron is used to flavor and color food and beverages. If infused for too long, the gin can take on medicinal flavor from the saffron, so taste after infusing for two days. The gin will acquire a slight oiliness from the saffron's natural oils.

1½ teaspoons saffron threads, crushed
One 750-ml bottle gin

Place the crushed saffron threads and gin in a clean jar or bottle with a tight lid or top. Shake a few times and store in a cool, dark place. Infuse for 2 to 3 days, making sure to shake the bottle once a day. When the infusion reaches the intensity you desire, strain and rebottle the infused gin.

LYCHEE-INFUSED VODKA

This subtle infusion is highly mixable and a great way to add an Asian flavor to cocktails.

10 lychees
One 750-ml bottle vodka

Place the lychees in a clean glass jar. Pour the vodka over the lychees and seal. Set aside to infuse from 3 to 4 days to 1 week, tasting periodically. Strain and rebottle the infused vodka.

Berry-Infused Gin

Hibiscus-Infused Vodka

Jasmine-Infused Vodka

Ginger-Infused Vodka

GINGER-INFUSED VODKA

This popular infusion is used in several cocktails. If you love the spicy flavor of ginger we recommend you allow the vodka to infuse two days. If you prefer something more restrained, infuse for 36 hours.

½ lb (250 g) fresh ginger, peeled and
    coarsely chopped
One 750-ml bottle vodka

Place ginger in vodka and let ginger infuse for 36 to 48 hours. Strain and rebottle the infused vodka.

JASMINE-INFUSED VODKA

This subtle, pale green infusion is used in The Cunning Kimono (page 36).

½ teaspoon of dried loose jasmine tea leaves
One 750-ml bottle vodka

Add the tea to the vodka. Set aside to infuse for 2 days, then strain and rebottle.

HIBISCUS-INFUSED VODKA

This red-colored infusion is one of the prettiest in this book and is very gratifying to make because the vodka changes color almost immediately.

2 teaspoons of dried Hibiscus Flowers
One 750-ml bottle vodka

Add the hibiscus flowers to the vodka and set aside to infuse for 3 days. Strain and rebottle the infused vodka.

PEPPER-INFUSED SHOCHU

This infusion has a nice peppery vegetal flavor that's only slightly spicy.

1 red bell pepper, sliced
½ medium-length chile, such as the finger
    chile, serrano or jalapeño, seeded and
    sliced
One 750-ml bottle shochu or soju

Place the sliced pepper and chile into a clean glass jar. Pour the shochu over the peppers, seal and set aside to infuse for 1 week. Strain and rebottle the infused shochu.

VANILLA BEAN–INFUSED RUM

This infusion should be tasted after four days to check the strength of the vanilla flavor as you don't want the vanilla to completely overwhelm the flavor of the rum. Vanilla beans are available at natural foods stores, gourmet stores or online.

4 vanilla beans
One 750-ml bottle aged rum

Split the vanilla beans lengthwise and scrape the seeds out. Add the seeds and pods to a bottle of rum and set aside to infuse for 4 to 5 days, shaking daily. Strain and rebottle the infused rum.

Vanilla Bean-Infused Rum

Lemongrass-
Infused Gin

chee-Infused
Vodka

Pepper-Infused
Shochu

Saffron-Infused Gin

Vodka & Shochu Cocktails

Late Blossom

VODKA HAS EXPERIENCED a meteoric rise in consumption in American homes and bars. After really only beginning to take off in the late 1940s, spurred on by the popularity of the then trendy Moscow Mule, vodka is now the single most popular liquor in the United States.

But what's not to like? Triple distilled from plants—usually grain or sometimes potato—vodka, by American definition, should have no distinctive flavor or aroma and be unaged. It should be made from a pure spirit with no additives except water, though small amounts of aromatics or other flavoring substances are permitted—ergo flavored vodkas. Finally, vodka is filtered, usually through charcoal, to remove any remaining impurities.

Vodka's neutral quality makes it supremely mixable and extremely receptive to flavorings, which opens up a world of creative possibilities for Asian cocktails. Flavored vodkas are nothing new—Russians have been making flavored vodkas for hundreds of years—but they only began to take hold in the American market in the 1980s when the first flavored vodkas were introduced. Now there are over a hundred flavors available. Some vodka producers, notably Hangar One, have responded to the growing interest in Asian flavors with infusions such as Mandarin Blossom Vodka, Wasabi Vodka, Kaffir Lime Vodka and others.

The most common form of Japanese shochu, called *korui* shochu, and the kindred spirit Korean soju, share many similarities with vodka. They are clear, unaged, multiple- or continuous-distilled spirits that are neutral in flavor and are highly mixable. Unlike vodka, both shochu and soju are relatively low in alcohol content (generally about 20 to 25 percent) and low in calories—making them attractive to health or diet-conscious drinkers. Nearly all of the Korean soju available in the West is this mild type.

Though practically any starchy ingredient with natural sugars can be used to make shochu or soju—there are hundreds of varieties available—all are distilled from fermented rice with one or more raw ingredients, depending on the desired style. Some of the most commonly used raw ingredients are rice, barley, wheat, buckwheat, potato and/or a variety of sweet potato.

The less common single-pot distillation method is sometimes used to make shochus, and less so sojus, that are distinct in flavor and aroma. These more expensive artisanal shochus, known as *honkaku* shochu (or historically *otsurui* shochu), retain most of the characteristics of the original raw material used to make them. Single-pot distilled shochus or sojus are typically aged and can be as high as 90 proof—though the most popular contain 25 percent alcohol. Honkaku shochu is traditionally enjoyed straight, on the rocks, or mixed with a bit of cold or hot water. Some mixologists, however, are using honkaku shochus as the base for creative cocktails. (In the recipes, we refer to single-pot distilled shochu by the primary raw material used; the multiple-distilled variety is referred to as simply "shochu" or "soju.")

Tranquility

This Asian twist on the classic American cooler known as "Arnold Palmer" or the "Country Club" is a great afternoon refresher. A soothing lemon-and-tea combo, Tranquility is a great counterpoint to spicy food. Thank you Buddakan!

1½ oz (45 ml) citrus (a.k.a. citron) vodka
1½ oz (45 ml) chilled Oolong Tea (see below)
½ oz (15 ml) freshly squeezed lemon juice
½ oz (15 ml) Lemongrass Syrup (page 20)
Lemon wedge, for garnish

Fill a highball glass with ice. Add the ingredients to an iced shaker and shake vigorously. Strain into a highball glass. Garnish with the lemon wedge and serve with a straw.

OOLONG TEA
1½ teaspoons loose-leaf oolong tea
½ cup (125 ml) boiling hot water

Combine the tea and boiling-hot water in a cup. Steep the tea for 5 to 8 minutes, then strain. Let cool before using.

The pom queen

If you love a well-made Cosmo, you'll love this nuanced cocktail. The original cocktail from Mie N Yu calls for Pama liqueur—a vodka-based spirit with pomegranate juice and a hint of tequila. We adapted it to use ingredients that you're more likely to have in your liquor cabinet or refrigerator. If you have Pama on hand, or want to try it, omit the grenadine and tequila, reduce the amount of vodka to 1½ ounces (45 ml) and use 1 ounce (30 ml) of Pama liqueur.

1¾ oz (52 ml) vodka
¾ oz (22 ml) Homemade Grenadine (page 21)
1 oz (30 ml) freshly squeezed orange juice
Splash of reposado or añejo tequila
1 oz (30 ml) chilled champagne
Lemon twist, for garnish

Combine all of the ingredients except the champagne in an iced shaker and shake vigorously. Strain into a chilled cocktail class and top with the champagne. Rub the rim of the glass with the lemon twist and drop into the glass.

The hanoi hooker

This amber-colored and deeply satisfying drink from Jeremy Shipley of Longrain Restaurant & Bar combines spicy ginger with undertones of caramel, apple and fresh pineapple—a hint of tropics in autumn.

One 1½-in (3.75-cm) piece fresh ginger, peeled and thinly sliced
One slice fresh pineapple, cut into 4 chunks
½ oz (15 ml) Simple Syrup (page 19)
1½ oz (45 ml) Ginger-Infused Vodka (page 23)
½ oz (15 ml) caramel syrup or Brown Sugar Syrup (page 19)
1 oz (30 ml) unfiltered apple juice or apple cider
½ oz (15 ml) freshly squeezed lime juice

Combine most of the ginger (reserve some for garnishing), the pineapple and Simple Syrup in a mixing glass, and muddle. Add ice and the remaining ingredients and shake vigorously. Double strain into a chilled cocktail glass and garnish with the reserved ginger slices.

Clockwise from the top: Tranquility,
The Hanoi Hooker, The Pom Queen

Lychee rose petal martini

The classic vodka cocktail lends itself perfectly to the luxurious sweetness of lychee and the aromatic subtlety of rose petals. When added to the glass, the weight of the rose syrup will cause it to sink to the bottom of the glass, creating a beautiful layered effect in this cocktail from The Cinnamon Club. Rose syrup can be bought made at home or bought in gourmet shops.

4 lychees
1½ oz (45 ml) vodka
½ oz (15 ml) store-bought or homemade Rose Syrup
  (page 20)
Rose petal, for garnish (optional)

In a mixing glass, muddle three of the lychees. Add ice and the vodka and shake vigorously. Double strain into a chilled cocktail glass. Add the Rose Syrup. Garnish with the fourth lychee and float the rose petal, if using, on the top of the cocktail.

Soho la

Like short skirts, this fashion-plate drink—combining creamy white lychees with hot pink watermelon—is meant for the hot days of summer. Serve with a straw and long-handled spoon to retrieve refreshing pieces of fruit. Warning: this delicious cocktail from Jeremy Shipley of Longrain Restaurant & Bar does not remotely taste of alcohol, making it easy to consume in quantity.

Four 1-in (2.5-cm) pieces fresh watermelon
4 lychees
½ oz (15 ml) Simple Syrup (page 19)
1½ oz (45 ml) Lychee-Infused Vodka (page 22)
½ oz (15 ml) lychee liqueur
Dash of freshly squeezed lime juice
3 oz (90 ml) unfiltered apple juice or apple cider

Combine the watermelon, lychees and Simple Syrup in a large collins glass, and muddle. Combine enough ice to fill a large collins glass and the remaining ingredients in a shaker and shake vigorously. Pour into a large collins glass and stir thoroughly. Add more ice if needed.

The white lily

In this cocktail from Morimoto, yuzu juice and sudachi shochu add a distinctive flavor to otherwise neutral-flavored Calpico. Sudachi shochu is shochu flavored with the sudachi citrus and molasses. If you can't find sudachi shochu, you can substitute mild-flavored shochu or soju with a splash of freshly squeezed lime juice.

2½ oz (75 ml) Sudachi shochu or either shochu or soju plus a splash of freshly squeezed lime juice
¼ oz (7 ml) bottled yuzu juice (unsalted)
¼ oz (7 ml) freshly squeezed lemon juice
1 oz (30 ml) Calpico
Lemon twist, for garnish

Combine the ingredients in an iced shaker and shake vigorously. Strain into a chilled cocktail glass. Garnish with the lemon twist.

The bombshell

Calpico is a concentrated yogurt drink that people in Japan often mix with different flavored carbonated and noncarbonated drinks. Here, it is combined with shochu and raspberry liqueur to produce a sweet, light cocktail that is full of flavor. We have Ariana Johnson of Modus to thank for this new shochu classic. Ariana prefers to use Ku Soju, which is made from sweet potatoes.

1½ oz (45 ml) soju or shochu
Approximately 3 oz (80 ml) Calpico
½ oz (15 ml) raspberry liqueur, such as Aqua Perfecta, or
    black raspberry liqueur, such as Chambord
3 raspberries, for garnish

Fill a collins glass with ice and add the soju. Add the Calpico to 1 inch (2.5 cm) from the top of the glass and stir thoroughly. Add the raspberry liqueur and stir briefly. Garnish with a spear of raspberries.

Green tea spritzer

This cool and refreshing tonic from Monsoon was inspired by the powerful antioxidant benefits of green tea. If your local liquor store doesn't carry Zen Green Tea Liqueur from Suntory, why not try one of the recipes for homemade green liqueur that can be found online?

1 oz (30 ml) vodka
½ oz (15 ml) Zen Green Tea Liqueur
Club soda, for topping

Fill a highball glass with ice. Add the vodka and green tea liqueur. Stir thoroughly. Top with soda water and stir briefly.

Green Tea Spritzer

Bloody mary, two ways

These Asian-inspired twists on this classic "eye-opener" will add a new dimension to your Sunday brunch fare.

GINGER MARY

3 slices peeled fresh ginger

$1/4$ teaspoon Szechuan peppercorns

2 oz (60 ml) Ginger-Infused Vodka (page 23)

4 oz (125 ml) tomato juice

2 dashes of Worcestershire sauce

$1/8$ teaspoon prepared horseradish

2 dashes of Maggi Seasoning

$1/2$ oz (15 ml) lemon juice

Lemon wheel, for garnish (optional)

In a mixing glass, muddle the ginger slices and Szechuan pepper until the peppercorns are crushed. Add ice and the rest of the ingredients and shake. Double-strain into an ice-filled Collins glass. Drop a lemon wheel in the drink for garnish, if using.

NOTE: Maggi Seasoning, created by Julius Maggi in Switzerland in the 1880s, is popular around the world, including Asia, where European colonists no doubt introduced it. Though made from a vegetable protein extract, it has meaty soy sauce–like flavor. It can be found in conventional grocery stores as well as Asian markets.

LEMONGRASS MARY

2 oz (60 ml) Lemongrass-Infused Vodka (page 22)

4 oz (125 ml) tomato juice

3 dashes of Worcestershire sauce

$1/4$ oz (7 ml) freshly squeezed lemon juice

$1/4$ oz (7 ml) tamarind concentrate (see page 17)

$1/8$ teaspoon Sriracha chili sauce

Pinch of salt and freshly ground black pepper

Lemon wheel, for garnish (optional)

Combine all the ingredients in an iced shaker. Shake and strain into an ice-filled Collins glass. Drop a lemon wheel in the drink for garnish, if using.

NOTE: Sriracha sauce is as ubiquitous in Southeast Asia as ketchup is in the United States—except that it's made with chiles. This spicy condiment is easy to find in Asian markets and health food stores with an Asian section. You can't miss it. There's a big rooster on the bottle.

asian cocktails

Late blossom

Bracing vodka combined with the delicate scent of orange blossoms give this subtle cocktail its enticing feminine strength. We have Kristen Johnson of Lantern to thank for this metro-sexual cocktail.

¼ oz (7 ml) orange blossom water
2 oz (60 ml) vodka
1 oz (30 ml) lychee juice
¼ oz (7 ml) Lillet Blanc
1 lychee, for garnish

Add the orange blossom water to a chilled cocktail glass, swirl and discard. In an iced shaker, combine the vodka, lychee juice and Lillet Blanc. Shake vigorously and strain into the cocktail glass. Garnish with the lychee.

Ping pong

This delightful and aromatic drink from Jeremy Shipley of Longrain Restaurant & Bar is hard to put down. Using fresh passion fruit lends an unbeatable freshness to this drink, and the black seeds look pretty in the glass. If you don't like passion fruit seeds—simply strain the pulp before adding it to the mixing glass. By the way, *citron* is simply the French word for "lemon"—not citrus.

4 canned lychees
1 tablespoon raw sugar
½ oz (15 ml) Simple Syrup (page 19) (omit if using bottled passion fruit juice)
2 tablespoons of fresh passion fruit pulp or 1 oz (30 ml) bottled passion fruit juice
1½ oz (45 ml) citrus (a.k.a. citron) vodka
½ oz (15 ml) lychee liqueur
Dash of freshly squeezed lime juice

Combine the lychees, raw sugar and the Simple Syrup, if using, in a mixing glass, and muddle. Add enough ice to fill a large rocks glass and the remaining ingredients. Shake vigorously and pour into a large rocks glass. Add more ice if needed.

The cunning kimono

The delicate floral notes of this pale green tinted libation from Kristen Johnson of Lantern is the perfect beverage to celebrate the arrival of spring. Enjoy it under a flowering cherry tree for added effect.

2 oz (60 ml) Jasmine-Infused Vodka (page 23)
1/2 oz (15 ml) Honey Syrup (page 20)
1/2 oz (15 ml) freshly squeezed lemon juice
1 edible flower, such as nasturtium, or lemon twist,
   for garnish (optional)

Combine all the ingredients (except the garnish) in an iced shaker. Shake vigorously and strain into a chilled cocktail glass. Garnish with the flower or lemon twist.

Hydrangea

This cocktail from Morimoto looks great in a cocktail glass. It combines elegance with the all-time favorite sweet-tart combo that's always a crowd pleaser. That's good thing because the recipe for Hydrangea Mix makes four drinks—the perfect excuse to invite some friends over. Its delicate purplish-pink color is reminiscent of hydrangea blossoms.

1/2 oz (15 ml) citrus (a.k.a. citron) vodka
2 1/2 oz (75 ml) Hydrangea Mix (recipe follows)
3/4 oz (22 ml) freshly squeezed lemon juice
Generous splash of black raspberry liqueur, such as
   Chambord
1 lychee, for garnish

Combine all the ingredients in an iced shaker and shake vigorously. Strain into a large chilled cocktail glass and garnish with the lychee.

HYDRANGEA MIX
Makes 10 oz (300 ml)
2 1/4 oz (67 ml) Lychee Syrup (page 21)
1 oz (30 ml) Calpico
1 oz (30 ml) Lillet Blanc
1 oz (30 ml) apple schnapps, such as DeKupyer Apple Barrel,
   or apple jack plus 1/2 teaspoon Simple Syrup (page 19)
3/4 oz (22 ml) Simple Syrup (page 19)
4 oz (120 ml) citrus (a.k.a. citron) vodka

Combine all of the ingredients and mix well. The mix will last in the refrigerator for a week.

The tokyo rose

Ginger adds a spicy touch to this Asian twist on the classic Cosmopolitan from Mie N Yu.

2¹⁄₂ oz (75 ml) Ginger-Infused Vodka (page 23)
¹⁄₂ oz (15 ml) Cointreau
1¹⁄₂ oz (45 ml) cranberry juice
Splash of freshly squeezed lime juice
One piece pickled ginger, for garnish

Combine all the ingredients in an iced shaker and shake vigorously. Strain into a chilled cocktail glass. Float a piece of pickled ginger on top of the cocktail.

From left to right: Hydrangea, The Tokyo Rose, The Cunning Kimono

The hibiscus petal

Hibiscus flowers give this cocktail from Kristen Johnson of Lantern its striking bright red color and help to soften the fiery spirit of vodka.

½ oz (15 ml) Simple Syrup (page 19)
½ oz (15 ml) freshly squeezed lime juice
6 fresh Thai basil leaves, torn, plus 1 sprig for garnish
½ oz (15 ml) freshly squeezed orange juice
2 oz (60 ml) Hibiscus-Infused Vodka (page 23)

Combine the Simple Syrup, lime juice and torn basil leaves in a mixing glass, and muddle. Add enough ice to fill a rocks glass, the orange juice and vodka. Shake vigorously and pour into a rocks glass. Add more ice if needed and garnish with the sprig of Thai basil.

Shiso-jito

The inspiration for this drink from Morimoto is the gingery Moscow Mule, which turned Americans on to the pleasures of vodka drinking in the late 1940s, and the Mojito, which features an abundance of fresh muddled mint—echoed in the fresh shiso.

3 fresh shiso leaves, torn into small pieces, or 2 leaves
   each fresh mint, Thai basil and coriander
$1/2$ oz (15 ml) freshly squeezed lime juice
1 tablespoon minced crystallized ginger candy
$1^1/2$ oz (45 ml) citrus (a.k.a. citron) vodka
Spicy ginger ale or beer, such as Reed's or Blenheim, for
   topping
Lime wedge, for garnish

Combine the shiso leaves, lime juice and candied ginger in a mixing glass, and muddle. Add enough ice to fill a highball glass and the vodka. Shake vigorously and pour into a highball glass. Add more ice if needed. Top with the ginger ale and stir briefly. Garnish with the lime wedge.

Kamikaze

The name of this bracing cocktail may come from the way it was originally drunk—a shot of vodka with a few drops of rose's lime juice and down the hatch. Though vodka is still front and center in this version, the addition of Cointreau softens the blow, allowing you to relieve your college drinking days with style.

2 oz (60 ml) vodka
1 teaspoon freshly squeezed lime juice
$1/2$ teaspoon Simple Syrup (page 19)
$1/2$ oz (15 ml) Cointreau

Fill a rocks glass with ice. Combine all the ingredients in an iced shaker and shake vigorously. Strain into the rocks glass.

Chi-So

Chi-so

In this exotic cocktail from SushiSamba, blood oranges, noted for their dark red color, are used to great effect. If blood oranges or tangerines are out of season, bottled tangerine juice can be used.

1 fresh shiso leaf or 1 leaf each fresh mint, basil and coriander (cilantro)
2 blood orange or tangerine segments, peeled and mem-
   branes removed, or $1/_4$ oz (7 ml) tangerine juice
2 teaspoons sugar
1 oz (30 ml) shochu or soju
1 oz (30 ml) orange-flavored vodka
1 oz (30 ml) freshly squeezed lime juice
1 oz (30 ml) orange juice
One orange or tangerine slice, for garnish

Fill a highball glass with ice. Combine the shiso, blood orange or tangerine segments or tangerine juice, and sugar in a mixing glass, and muddle. Add ice and the remaining ingredients and shake vigorously. Strain into the highball glass and garnish with the orange or tanger-ine slice.

The chucumber

The refreshing flavor of cucumber plays a starring role in this pleasantly tart cocktail from SushiSamba. It's a perfect choice for a summer evening. Mugi and kome are mildly aromatic honkaku-style shochus. If you can't find them, use a korui-style shochu or soju.

2 thick slices of Japanese or "baby" cucumber or 1 thick
   slice of English cucumber
2 teaspoons sugar
2 oz (60 ml) mugi or kome shochu
$1/_2$ oz (15 ml) Licor 43
1 oz (30 ml) freshly squeezed lime juice
2 paper thin slices of Japanese or "baby" cucumber or
   1 paper thin slice of English cucumber, for garnish

Combine the cucumber and sugar in a mixing glass, and muddle gently. Add ice and the remaining ingredi-ents and shake vigorously. Strain into a chilled cocktail glass. Float the cucumber slices on the cocktail.

The jade fox

This twist on a Collins from Ariana Johnson of Modus lets the ingredients speak for themselves. The sugar and the kiwiberries are sweet and sour, and shochu takes the place of gin. Kiwiberries have a similar flavor to regular kiwis, but with a guavalike note. If substituting peeled kiwi, add a splash of apple juice to soften the tartness. This cocktail is low in alcohol and is perfect when you're looking for something light and refreshing. Ariana prefers to use Ku Soju, which is made from sweet potatoes.

4 to 5 kiwi berries or two ¼-in (6-mm) slices peeled kiwi,
   plus extra for garnish
2 to 3 teaspoons sugar
1 oz (30 ml) soju or shochu
Splash of apple juice, if using kiwi slices (optional)
Club soda, for topping

Combine the kiwi berries or kiwi slices and sugar in a mixing glass, and muddle. Add enough ice to fill a collins glass and the soju and apple juice, if using. Shake vigorously and pour into a collins glass. Add more ice if necessary. Top with club soda and stir briefly. Garnish with a kiwi berry or a slice of kiwi.

Spiked lemongrass lemonade

One sip of this new classic thirst-quencher and you'll be ready to hit the lawn with your croquet mallet in hand (or bocce balls, if that's your pleasure). We have Starry Night Café to thank for his perfect summer drink.

2 oz (60 ml) citrus (a.k.a. citron) vodka
¼ oz (7 ml) freshly squeezed lemon juice
1 oz (30 ml) Lemongrass Syrup (page 20)
Splash of club soda
Lemon twist, for garnish

In a shaker, add the vodka, lemon juice and Lemongrass Syrup and enough ice to fill a highball glass. Shake vigorously and pour into a highball glass. Add more ice if necessary. Top with club soda and stir briefly. Garnish with the lemon twist.

From left to right: The Red Geisha, The Silk Road, Spiked Lemongrass Lemonade

The red geisha

This drink's strawberry color and candied ginger taste might take you back to your early days of Shirley Temple imbibing, but this delicious cocktail is all adult. To keep things from getting too sweet, this drink from Kristen Johnson of Lantern is topped off with spicy ginger beer (Blenheim or Reed's are good choices)—something you surely wouldn't have cared for in your Shirley Temple.

2 to 3 strawberries, sliced
1 oz (30 ml) Ginger Syrup (page 19)
2 oz (60 ml) vodka
½ oz (15 ml) freshly squeezed lime juice
Splash of spicy ginger ale or beer, such as Reed's or
  Blehneim
One slice each of lime and strawberry, for garnish

In a mixing glass, muddle the strawberries and Ginger Syrup. Add enough ice to fill a rocks glass, the vodka and lime juice, and shake vigorously. Pour into a rocks glass. Add more ice if needed. Top with the ginger ale and stir briefly. Garnish with the slice of lime and strawberry.

The silk road

Peaches were long considered to have their origins in Persia, but it is now generally thought that they originated in China, making their way to the Mediterranean with trades along the Silk Road. In this aptly named cocktail from Timothy Lacey of Spring, a delicate mixture of aromatic flavors creates an exotic drink that balances sweet and dry like nobody's business.

15 fresh Thai basil leaves
Splash of Simple Syrup (page 19)
Pinch of kosher salt or sea salt
1½ oz (45 ml) vodka
½ oz (15 ml) Lillet Blanc
½ oz (15 ml) crème de pêche, such as Briottet, or peach
  schnapps
Splash of freshly squeezed lime juice
Club soda, for topping

Combine the basil, Simple Syrup and salt in a rocks glass, and muddle. Add ice and the remaining ingredients, except the club soda, and stir thoroughly. Add the club soda and stir briefly.

Rum & Tequila Cocktails

Cyclone

IF YOU'VE EVER PARTAKEN of the sacred rite of a shot of tequila combined with salt and a lime wedge, you can appreciate the wisdom of George Carlin's "One tequila, two tequila, three tequila, floor." Outside of Mexico, tequila's fraternity-house association has given way to a new appreciation for Mexico's national drink, which can be wonderfully assertive or be as smooth and mellow as the finest sipping brandy.

Tequila, which is made from the heart of the blue agave plant in the region of Jalisco, Mexico, can be divided into three major categories. The first is silver tequila, also called "blanco" or "plato," which is bottled immediately after the heart is fermented and distilled. Reposados, or "rested" tequilas, are aged for two to twelve months in oak barrels. Next are the sipping tequilas—the añejos, which means "aged." They are aged in oak barrels for at least one year but are typically aged three to five years. When buying tequila look for 100% agave on the label for the best tequila. Avoid gold tequila—it is unaged silver tequila that has been colored and flavored with caramel.

We love the strong vegetal flavor of silver tequila, but if you're not a fan, try the softer reposado in cocktails. Traditionally, aged tequila has not been used for mixing, though a new generation of mixologists are using it to create smooth, luxurious cocktails (see Mango Margarita created by Mexican-born mixologist Migual Aranda).

Whereas tequila's introduction to the United States dates only to the late 1940s, when the newly created Margarita popularized it, rum's place in the American liquor cabinet goes back centuries. First distilled on the sugarcane plantations of the Caribbean in the seventeenth century, rum's popularity soon spread to Colonial America. To support the demand for the drink, the first rum distillery in the colonies was set up in 1664 on present-day Staten Island. Colonial New Englanders manufactured rum using West Indian molasses, creating what became the largest and most prosperous industry in the region. Today rum is made primarily in the Caribbean, where the climate is ideal for growing sugar cane, and secondarily in South America, though there are rums made in other parts of the world as well.

Distilled from fermented sugar cane juice or more frequently molasses, rum can be divided into four main categories: white, amber, dark (a.k.a. light, medium and heavy), and aged (añejo) rum. Aged rum, which has a tawny color and more mellow flavor, must be aged at least six years, whereas the other rums are aged between six months and up to six years, but most are aged between one and three years. Rum bottles must, by law, state their country of origin, where slightly different fermenting, distilling and aging methods render basic styles of rum—lighter or heavier-bodied, clear or colored—for which the country is known.

Cyclone

A play on the classic Hurricane, whose signature ingredient is passion fruit juice, this slightly spicy Indian-inspired cocktail should help you ride out any storm that comes your way. We got the idea of combining sweet fruit with spicy chiles from Shubhra Ramenini's recipe for Fruit Chaat (www.enticewithspice.com). If you cannot find fresh passion fruit or bottled passion fruit juice, substitute a fruit juice blend that contains passion fruit. If the blend contains mango juice, use $3/4$ ounce (22 ml) of mango juice and $1^1/_4$ ounces (37 ml) of the fruit blend. If monotonous rains are keeping you holed up by the bar, try a calming variation on this cocktail called the "Monsoon." To create the Monsoon, replace the cumin seeds, chili pepper and salt with 4 cardamom pods. (Be sure to muddle the pods until they break.)

Two 1-inch (2.5-cm) chunks fresh pineapple
2 teaspoons sugar
Scant $1/4$ teaspoon cumin seeds, toasted
2 slices of finger, serrano or jalapeño chile (with seeds)
Pinch of kosher salt or sea salt
$1^1/_4$ oz (37 ml) light rum
$3/4$ oz (22 ml) dark rum
$1/2$ oz (15 ml) freshly squeezed lime juice
1 oz (30 ml) mango juice
1 oz (30 ml) passion fruit juice or 2 tablespoons fresh passion fruit pulp (from 1 passion fruit)
Splash of grenadine (see page 21)
Pineapple wedge, for garnish

Fill a collins glass with ice. Place the pineapple, sugar, toasted cumin seeds, chili pepper slices and salt in a mixing glass, and muddle. (You should press hard enough to crush the cumin seeds.) Add ice and the rest of the ingredients. Shake vigorously and double strain into the collins glass. Garnish with the pineapple wedge.

NOTE: To toast cumin seeds, place the seed in a small skillet over medium-low heat. Stir frequently. When the seeds start to remove an aroma and become lightly browned, remove from the heat.

Shanghai

This pretty pink cocktail makes a nice after dinner drink. Anisette, a clear very sweet liquor that is made with anise seeds, is similar in flavor to star anise, a favorite spice in China, which no doubt inspired the drink's name. The preferred choice of rum for this classic cocktail is Jamaican light rum.

2 oz (60 ml) light rum
1 oz (30 ml) anisette
1 oz (30 ml) freshly squeezed lemon juice
1 teaspoon grenadine

Combine the ingredients in an iced shaker and shake vigorously. Strain into a chilled cocktail glass.

Shanghai

Daiquiri, three ways

The original daiquiri hails from Cuba and is quite simple—rum, lime juice and sugar. Our three Asian twists are also equally simple and delicious—from the aromatic Thai Basil Daiquiri, to the earthy yet sour Tamarind Daiquiri to the delicate golden-colored Calamansi Daiquiri.

THAI BASIL DAIQUIRI

1$\frac{1}{2}$ oz (45 ml) white rum
$\frac{3}{4}$ oz (22 ml) Thai Basil Syrup (page 21)
$\frac{1}{2}$ oz (15 ml) freshly squeezed lime juice

Combine the ingredients in an iced shaker and shake vigorously. Strain into a chilled cocktail glass.

TAMARIND DAIQUIRI

1$\frac{1}{2}$ oz (45 ml) white rum
$\frac{3}{4}$ oz (22 ml) Simple Syrup (page 19)
$\frac{1}{2}$ oz (15 ml) tamarind concentrate (see page 17)

Combine the ingredients in an iced shaker and shake vigorously. Strain into a chilled cocktail glass.

CALAMANSI DAIQUIRI

1$\frac{1}{2}$ oz (45 ml) white rum
$\frac{3}{4}$ oz (22 ml) Simple Syrup (page 19)
$\frac{1}{2}$ oz plus $\frac{3}{4}$ teaspoon (20 ml) defrosted frozen or freshly
    squeezed calamansi juice

Combine the ingredients in an iced shaker and shake vigorously. Strain into a chilled cocktail glass.

NOTE: Calamansi juice is also available presweetened in bottles. If you use this, reduce the amount of simple syrup accordingly.

The Orchid

The orchid

The vanilla bean, which is harvested from a very special variety of orchid (out of 20,000 possible orchid varieties!), is the inspiration for this honey-colored cocktail from Timothy Lacey of Spring. Aged rum is infused with vanilla, giving this drink a heady aroma and distinctive flavor that works equally well before or after dinner.

2$\frac{1}{2}$ oz (75 ml) Vanilla Bean–Infused Rum (page 23)
$\frac{1}{4}$ oz (7 ml) each yuzu juice and freshly squeezed lemon
    juice or $\frac{1}{2}$ oz (15 ml) freshly squeezed lemon juice
$\frac{1}{2}$ oz (15 ml) Simple Syrup (page 19)
Fresh orchid blossom or small lemon twist, for garnish

Combine the ingredients in an iced shaker. Shake vigorously and strain into a chilled cocktail glass. Garnish with the orchid blossom or lemon twist.

Mai tai

Invented in 1944 by Victor "Trader Vic" Bergeron, this island concoction is a mainstay at tiki lounges and Chinese-American restaurants—along with drinks like the Scorpion or Pink Lady. The original Mai Tai recipe was made with aged rum. Many recipes are made with light and dark rum and include pineapple juice and orange juice. Except for a touch of dark rum to deepen the rum flavor, this version is fairly close to the spirit of the original, where lime juice is the only fruit used. Trader Vic used Rock Candy syrup in the original Mai Tai. We use the easier-to-find cane syrup, which is more flavorful than plain 'ole simple syrup.

2 oz (60 ml) aged rum
1 oz (30 ml) freshly squeezed lime juice
³/₄ oz (22 ml) Cointreau
¹/₄ oz (7 ml) cane syrup or 2:1 Simple Syrup (page 19)
¹/₄ oz (7 ml) orgeat or almond syrup
¹/₂ teaspoon dark rum
Orange slice and maraschino cherry for garnish

Fill a large rocks glass with crushed ice. Combine the ingredients in an iced shaker and shake vigorously. Strain into the rocks glass and add the garnish.

The thai coconut

This tropical-tasting cocktail from Starry Night Café has one of the most inventive and playful garnishes around. Coconut rum can be a bit cloying on its own, but freshly squeezed lime juice balances it nicely in this drink. The staff at Starry Night recommend Bacardi coconut rum—and they think it just might make a convert out of you, too.

2 oz (60 ml) coconut rum
³/₄ oz (22 ml) Lemongrass Syrup (page 20)
1 oz (30 ml) freshly squeezed lime juice
Candied Lemongrass Straws, for garnish (recipe follows)

Fill a rocks glass with ice. Combine the ingredients in an iced shaker and shake vigorously. Strain into the rocks glass and serve with a candied lemongrass straw.

CANDIED LEMONGRASS STRAWS
Makes approximately 15 straws
1 fresh stalk lemongrass
1 cup (250 ml) 2:1 Simple Syrup (page 19)
Sugar, preferably demerara, for coating

Wash the lemongrass and cut about ¹/₂ inch (1.25 cm) off the hard root end and the top one-third off the stalk, and discard. Remove the tough outer layers and discard. Cut the stalk in half lengthwise. Make a slit down the middle of the stalk and unravel the layers into hollow tubes. In a small saucepan, combine the lemongrass straws and enough 2:1 Simple Syrup to cover. Bring to a boil and boil for 15 minutes. Remove from the heat strain the lemongrass straws, retaining the Simple Syrup. Let the lemongrass and syrup cool separately for about 15 minutes and then recombine them. Repeat the boiling and cooling process four to five times, letting the lemongrass cool and dry out between sessions so that it retains more sugar with each boil. When the lemongrass straws have cooled, roll in granulated sugar (preferably demerara) and place on a baking sheet in a warm oven (175°F/80°C) to dry, about 25 minutes. Let cool before using.

asian cocktails

Tamarind margarita

Sour tamarind replaces the lime in this margarita, giving it a softer less acidic balance of sweet and sour.

1½ oz (45 ml) silver tequila
½ oz (15 ml) freshly squeezed orange juice
½ oz (15 ml) triple sec
½ oz (15 ml) tamarind concentrate (see page 17)

Fill a rocks glass with ice. Combine the ingredients in an iced shaker and shake vigorously. Strain into the rocks glass.

Clockwise from left: Mai Tai,
Tamarind Margarita, The Thai Coconut

Mango margarita

Here mixologist Miguel Aranda has added mango to the basic margarita trinity—orange, lime and tequila—bringing it to new heights. The sweet flavor of mango is fantastic paired with smoky Mezcal, the woody flavor of aged tequila and spicy chili salt. Unlike tequila, mezcal can be made with agave other than the famous "blue" agave and is produced throughout most of Mexico—not just Jalisco. When making mezcal, the agave hearts are baked in underground ovens heated with wood charcoal, which gives Mezcal its distinctive smoky taste. Rested or silver tequila can be used, though aged is best for this revisionist margarita.

Chili Salt, for rimming (recipe follows)
1 1/2 oz (45 ml) mango juice
1/2 oz (15 ml) freshly squeezed lime juice
1/2 oz (15 ml) Cointreau
Dash of mezcal (optional)
1 1/2 oz (45 ml) tequila, preferably añejo (aged)

Rim a rock glass and set aside. In a shaker, add enough ice to fill a rocks glass and the ingredients. Shake vigorously and pour into the rimmed rock glass. Add more ice if needed.

CHILI SALT
1 medium-length dried red chile or 1 chipotle, coarsely chopped
1 tablespoon kosher or sea salt

In a mortar, grind the chopped dried chile. Add the salt to it and stir to combine.

NOTE: For an extra smoky flavor, make the Chili Salt with a chipotle, which is a dried, smoked jalapèno.

Enlightenment

In this Asian-inspired margarita from Buddakan the pronounced vegetal flavor of silver tequila is enhanced by the refreshing and cooling cucumber—the perfect counterpoint to the pleasantly spicy simple syrup.

2 oz (60 g) piece Japanese, "baby," or English cucumber, ends trimmed
2 oz (60 ml) silver tequila
3/4 oz (37 ml) triple sec
3/4 oz (37 ml) equal parts fresh lemon and lime juice
1 oz (30 ml) Thai Chili Syrup (page 21)
2 or 3 cucumber wheels or a cucumber spear, for garnish

Peel the cucumber piece in strips (leaving half the skin on). Coarsely chop the cucumber and place in a food processor or blender. Pulse on low speed until crushed. Fill a rocks glass with ice. Place 2 tablespoons of the fresh crushed cucumber and the rest of the ingredients in an iced shaker. Shake vigorously and strain into the rocks glass. If serving in a margarita glass, place a cucumber wheel on the rim of the glass. Garnish with 2 or 3 cucumber wheels on a cocktail pick or with a 4-inch (10-cm)-long cucumber spear.

Ginger basil margarita

In this Asian-inspired Margarita from Jujube, spicy-sweet Ginger Syrup and distinctive Thai basil blends perfectly with the assertive flavor of silver tequila. Chocolate basil is a nice substitute for Thai basil in this refreshing drink.

3 to 5 fresh Thai basil leaves, plus 1 sprig for garnish
1 oz (30 ml) silver tequila
½ oz (15 ml) freshly squeezed orange juice
½ oz (15 ml) triple sec
½ oz (15 ml) freshly squeezed lime juice
1 oz (30 ml) Ginger Syrup (page 19)
Lime wedge, for garnish

Combine the basil leaves with two cubes of ice in a mixing glass, and muddle. Add enough ice to fill a rocks glass and the remaining ingredients and shake vigorously. Pour into a rocks glass and add additional ice if needed. Garnish with the sprig of Thai basil and/or the wedge of lime.

Clockwise from left: Ginger Basil Margarita, Enlightenment, Mango Margarita

From left to right: Mango Mojito, Scorpion

Mango mojito

This Asian twist on a Latin classic from the Cinnamon Club introduces sweetness of mango without diminishing the refreshing taste of citrus and mint. Mango syrup has an intensity of mango flavor that can't be duplicated, but don't hesitate to make this mojito if you don't have any on hand. Simply add an additional $1/4$ ounce (7 ml) of mango juice and a splash of simple syrup. It will still be delicious.

3 lime wedges
$1/2$ teaspoon demerara sugar or other raw sugar
5 to 7 fresh mint leaves, plus 1 sprig of mint for garnish
$1^3/4$ oz (50 ml) white rum
2 teaspoons mango syrup
1 oz (30 ml) mango juice
Club soda, for topping
Mango slice, for garnish (optional)

Fill a collins glass with crushed ice. Squeeze the lime wedges over a mixing glass, then drop in the squeezed wedges. Add the sugar and mint leaves, and muddle. Add ice, the rum, mango syrup and mango juice. Shake vigorously and strain into the collins glass. Top with club soda and stir briefly. Garnish with the sprig of mint and mango slice, if using. Serve with a straw.

Scorpion

The sting of this classic tiki bar favorite is soothed by the sweetness of almond-flavored orgeat syrup and orange juice. This drink may bring back memories of your favorite neighborhood Chinese-American restaurant—the type that offers grilled cheese on the kid's menu and that is perhaps sadly a dying breed.

1 oz (30 ml) light rum
$3/4$ oz (22 ml) brandy
$1/2$ oz (15 ml) orgeat or almond syrup
$1^1/4$ oz (37 ml) freshly squeezed orange juice
$3/4$ oz (22 ml) freshly squeezed lemon juice
$1/2$ oz (15 ml) Simple Syrup (page 19)
$1/2$ oz (15 ml) 151 rum
Orange slice and maraschino cherry, for garnish

Fill a collins glass with ice. Combine all of the ingredients, except the 151 rum, in an ice-filled shaker. Shake vigorously and strain into the collins glass. Top with the 151 rum and add the garnish.

Gin Cocktails

From the top: Nashi Cocktail, Asian Negroni

"SHUT UP AND DRINK YOUR GIN!" is Fagin's response to a boy in the 1968 movie *Oliver* based on Dickens' *Oliver Twist*. Though shocking to us today, this comment is rooted in the historically checkered relationship between the Dutch-born liquor and the English, with whom it is so strongly identified. The spirit's migration to England from Holland came about when in 1688 the king of England, William III (a Dutchman), imposed heavy tariffs on French wine and brandy, making gin very attractive. Soon English distillers began making gin themselves, making it even more affordable, and very popular among the poor. Its consumption became so widespread that the first half of the eighteenth century was known as the "gin craze," a period of extreme drunkenness, particularly in London.

A neutral-grain spirit flavored with botanicals, juniper chief among them, gin has a highly distinctive taste and aroma. In fact the name gin comes from the Dutch word for juniper—*jenever* —or possibly from the French word for juniper— *genievre*. Like many spirits or fortified wines flavored with botanicals, the original raison d'être of gin was medicinal. In the seventeenth century a Dutch doctor combined alcohol and the blueish green berries for the purpose of remedying kidney aliments. Though the good doctor's experiment didn't work, his "tonic" became the basis for many classics behind the bar—the Gimlet, the Singapore Sling, the Tom Collins, and of course the Cocktail.

Today the most popular type of gin on the market is London dry gin. The name denotes a style rather than locale of distillation—it can be made anywhere. Dry gins may be flavored with as many as ten botanicals, such coriander seeds, lemon and orange peels, fennel, cassia, anise, almond, angelica, cinnamon or others. Plymouth gin, made by only one distiller, is a full-bodied, slightly fruity cousin of London dry gin. Unlike London dry gin, it is site specific: it must be made in Plymouth, England. Less popular today, and therefore harder to find, are the older sweeter-style gins that are flavored with fewer botanicals than dry gin (but always juniper!): Genever gins (a.k.a. "Hollands" gin or "Dutch" gin), which have a distinct flavor from the malted barley used in their distillation and, if aged, from the time they spent in oak barrels; and Old Tom, which is said to have been the gin used in the original Tom Collins. All of the cocktails in this book are made with the ubiquitous dry-style gin, including Plymouth, if that is your preference.

Nashi cocktail

This pale golden cocktail from Timothy Lacey of Spring was inspired by the delicate flavor of Asian pears, called *nashi.* Surprise your guests with a unique rimmer of dehydrated honey granules, or try whole cane sugar or demerara sugar for an interesting touch. The honey granules can be ground to a finer texture, if you prefer. Whole cane sugar or demerara sugar can be found at natural foods stores.

Honey granules, whole cane sugar, or demerara sugar, for
 rimming
1½ oz (45 ml) gin
1½ oz (45 ml) sake
1 oz (30 ml) pear liqueur
Pinch of kosher salt or sea salt
Splash of freshly squeezed lemon juice
Splash of Simple Syrup (page 19)

Rim a chilled cocktail glass in the honey granules. Combine the ingredients in an iced shaker and shake vigorously. Strain into the rimmed glass.

Lemongrass gimlet

This Asian twist on the gin gimlet from Miguel Aranda takes the classic cocktail to new realms. As the lemongrass infuses the gin, its grassy characteristic becomes more pronounced, which perfectly compliments the herbal notes in gin.

½ oz (15 ml) Lemongrass Puree (recipe follows)
1½ oz (45 ml) Lemongrass-Infused Gin (page 22)
1½ oz (45 ml) gin
½ oz (15 ml) Simple Syrup (page 19)
1 egg white

Combine all the ingredients in an iced shaker and shake with extra enthusiasm. Strain into a chilled cocktail glass.

LEMONGRASS PUREE
Makes ¾ cup (200 ml)
2 stalks fresh lemongrass
¼ cup (60 ml) 2:1 Simple Syrup (page 19)
¼ cup (60 ml) water
¼ cup (60 ml) freshly squeezed lemon juice

Wash the lemongrass and cut about 1½ inches (3.75 cm) off the hard root ends and the top one-third off the stalks, and discard. Remove the tough outer layers and discard. Bruise the tender white stalks with the broad side of a chef's knife. Coarsely chop the stalks and combine them with the 2:1 Simple Syrup, the water and the lemon juice in a blender or a food processor. Puree until smooth and strain the liquid into a clean container. Any unused puree will keep in a sealed container in the refrigerator for one week.

Lemongrass Gimlet

Hokkaido cocktail

This three-ingredient cocktail, presumably named after Hokkaido, Japan, is perfect in its simplicity. And its balanced mix of flavors turns out to be the Asian equivalent of the original martini, which was made with gin, a great deal more vermouth than the modern cocktail, and with orange bitters. If you're substituting Cointreau for triple sec, add a splash of simple syrup.

1½ oz (45 ml) gin
1 oz (30 ml) sake
½ oz (15 ml) triple sec

Combine all the ingredients in an iced shaker and shake vigorously. Strain into a chilled cocktail glass.

Fool's Gold

Hokkaido Cocktail

Fool's gold

This elegant cocktail from The Cinnamon Club was created with decadence in mind. Its color—rich golden yellow tinged with glowing red—is reminiscent of the setting sun. Gabriel Boudier Saffron Gin is the only saffron gin on the market. If you can't find it, you can infuse a batch at home using a dry London-style gin. This cocktail works equally well with fruit-infused gin. Blueberries, raspberries or peach with lemongrass are good combinations (see page 22).

2 cardamom pods
1¾ oz (22 ml) Saffron-Infused Gin (page 22)
½ oz (15 ml) crème de mûre, or blackberry syrup, or crème de cassis
2 teaspoons Simple Syrup (page 19)
½ oz (15 ml) freshly squeezed lime juice
One gold leaf, broken into pieces, for garnish (optional)

Place one of the cardamom pods in a mixing glass, and muddle until crushed. Add ice, the gin, crème de mûre, Simple Syrup and lime juice. Shake vigorously and double strain into a chilled cocktail glass. Garnish with remaining cardamom pod and the flecks of gold leaf, if using.

Blue Basil

Asian negroni

This Negroni from Miguel Aranda is one that everyone can get behind—Campari lovers and naysayers alike. The classic Negroni is made with equal parts gin, sweet vermouth and the bitter deep-red Italian aperitif, creating quite a bracing drink. Here, the addition of tangerine juice and the use of a relatively small amount of Campari—used more like, well, bitters—makes for a more mellow variation on the Negroni. The frothy egg white adds a velvety texture and festive topping. If tangerines aren't in season, bottled tangerine juice will suffice. Or use fresh-squeezed orange juice instead.

1½ oz (45 ml) gin
½ oz (15 ml) sweet vermouth
½ oz (15 ml) tangerine juice
¼ oz (15 ml) Campari
¼ oz (15 ml) sake
One egg white
Tangerine or orange twist, for garnish

Combine the ingredients and enough ice to fill a large rocks glass in shaker. Shake with extra enthusiasm and pour into a large rocks glass. Add more ice if needed. Garnish with the tangerine or orange twist.

Blue basil

The connection between kitchen and bar is stronger than ever—look no further than the abundance of fresh ingredients and exotic spices and aromatics in the cocktails in this book. John Blue of the Vietnamese restaurant Sapa in NYC, now sadly closed, dreamt up this stiff cocktail while enjoying spicy beef soup with sprouts and Thai basil during a break from the bar. The gin of choice for this cocktail is Magellan, which has a naturally blue cast to it from iris. Bombay gin or any other dry gin will work—the drink just won't have an arresting blue color.

3 lime wedges
6 to 8 fresh Thai basil leaves, plus 1 sprig for garnish
¾ oz (22 ml) Simple Syrup (page 19)
2¼ oz (67 ml) gin
¾ oz (22 ml) freshly squeezed lime juice
Splash of club soda
Lime wheel, for garnish

Combine the lime wedges, basil leaves and Simple Syrup in a mixing glass, and muddle. Add enough ice to fill a large rocks glass and the gin and lime juice. Shake vigorously and pour into a large rocks glass. Add more ice if needed. Top with the club soda and stir briefly. Garnish with the lime wheel and the sprig of basil.

Coriander collins

This simple cocktail from the Lab Bar is a twist on one of the oldest classics around. Its cool green color makes it a perfect summer refresher. Try using the vanilla sugar as a rimmer for other cocktails.

Leaves from 2 sprigs fresh coriander (cilantro), plus 1 sprig
   for garnish
3 teaspoons vanilla sugar, store-bought or homemade
   (recipe follows)
2 oz (52 ml) gin
1 oz (30 ml) freshly squeezed lemon juice
Club soda, for topping

Fill a small collins glass with ice. Combine the coriander leaves and vanilla sugar in a mixing glass, and muddle. Add ice, the gin and the lemon juice. Shake vigorously and double strain into the collins glass. Top with club soda and stir briefly. Garnish with the remaining sprig of coriander.

VANILLA SUGAR
Makes $\frac{1}{2}$ pound (250 g)
1 large vanilla bean, seeded and chopped
$\frac{1}{2}$ lb (250 g) sugar

Scrap the seeds from the vanilla pods and set aside. Coarsely chop the seeded pods. Place the seeds, chopped pods and sugar in a large food processor and process until thoroughly combined. Let the mixture rest for 20 to 25 minutes. Pour the infused sugar through a sieve to remove the larger pieces of vanilla. Store in a glass jar with a tight lid.

The sensei

This pleasantly vegetal cocktail from Miguel Aranda is especially enjoyable sitting next to a pool on a hot summer evening. While you don't have to have those stars aligned to enjoy this cocktail, Miguel suggests you give it a try. This cocktail was created with Hendrix gin in mind but any dry London-style gin such as Gordon's or Tangueray can be used. Miguel's sensei for this cocktail is cocktailian Cesar Ortiz of Town (NYC).

4 thin slices Japanese or "baby" cucumber or 2 thin slices
   English cucumber, plus additional slices for garnish
$\frac{1}{2}$ oz (15 ml) Pepper-Infused Shochu (page 23)
$3\frac{1}{2}$ oz (75 ml) gin
$\frac{1}{4}$ oz (15 ml) Simple Syrup (page 19)
$1\frac{1}{2}$ oz (45 ml) freshly squeezed lime juice
Club soda, for topping

Place the cucumber slices in a mixing glass, and muddle. Add enough ice to fill a highball glass, the Pepper-infused Shochu, gin, Simple Syrup and lime juice. Shake vigorously and pour into a highball glass. Add more ice if needed. Top with the club soda and stir briefly. Garnish with the remaining cucumber slices.

The junebug

An Asian twist on the traditional Pimm's Cup, this refreshing summer drink from Kristen Johnson of Lantern gets a spicy-sweet kick with homemade ginger syrup.

4 to 5 slices Japanese or "baby" cucumber or 3 slices English (hothouse) cucumber
$\frac{1}{2}$ oz (15 ml) freshly squeezed lemon juice
$\frac{1}{2}$ oz (15 ml) Ginger Syrup (page 19)
2 oz (15 ml) Pimm's No. 1 Cup
Spicy ginger ale, such as Reed's or Blenheim
Lemon wheel, for garnish

Place the cucumber slices in a large collins or pilsner glass and fill with ice. In an iced shaker, combine the lemon juice, ginger syrup and Pimm's No. 1 Cup. Shake vigorously and strain into the collins or pilsner glass. Top with the ginger ale and stir briefly. Garnish with the lemon wheel.

NOTE: A Zombie glass, or any glass with about 14-ounce (420-ml) capacity, will work for this cocktail.

From left to right: The Sensei,
The Junebug, Coriander Collins

Lychee gimlet

The herbaceous quality of gin compliments the sweet flavor of lychees in this gimlet from Starry Night Café. For a sweeter version, make this drink with the syrup from a can of lychees. The ideal gin for this cocktail is Beefeater or Tangueray, but any dry London-style gin will do.

2 oz (60 ml) gin
1/2 oz (15 ml) triple sec
1 oz (30 ml) lychee juice
1/4 oz (7 ml) freshly squeezed lime juice
1 lychee, for garnish

Combine all the ingredients in an iced shaker and shake vigorously. Strain into a chilled cocktail glass and garnish with the lychee.

Singapore sling

This deservedly famous drink is incredibly refreshing—fruity but not cloying. It was invented by Ngiam Tong Boon in 1915 for the Long Bar at Raffles Hotel in Singapore, and in the early years after its creation it was sometimes referred to as the "Straights Sling." Various recipes abound—each claiming to be the original. This version is very close to the original as put forth by the Raffles Hotel—which claims that Peter Heering's cherry liqueur is a key ingredient in an authentic Singapore Sling. (You can find their recipe on the Raffles Hotel website.)

1 1/2 oz (45 ml) gin
2 1/2 oz (75 ml) pineapple juice
1/2 oz (15 ml) freshly squeezed lime juice
1/2 oz (15 ml) Cherry Heering
1/4 oz (7 ml) Bénédictine
1/4 oz (7 ml) Cointreau
Dash of Angostura bitters
Club soda, for topping

Fill a large collins glass with ice. Combine all the ingredients, except the club soda, in an iced shaker and shake vigorously. Strain into the collins glass. Top with the club soda and stir briefly.

Kashmiri iced tea

Kashmiri chai tea, which blends black tea with spices such as saffron, cinnamon, cardamom and cloves, is the inspiration for this lightly alcoholic cocktail from Monsoon. For a sweeter drink, use triple sec instead of Cointreau.

4 1/2 oz (140 ml) chilled Kashmiri tea
3/4 oz (22 ml) gin
3/4 oz (22 ml) Cointreau
Splash of freshly squeezed lemon juice
Lemon wheel, for garnish

Fill a highball glass with ice. Add the ingredients and stir thoroughly. Garnish with the lemon wheel.

KASHMIRI TEA
Makes 1 cup (250 ml) tea
1 cup (250 ml) boiling hot water
1 1/2 teaspoons loose-leaf Kashmiri chai tea

Combine the tea and boiling-hot water in a cup. Steep the tea for 3 to 5 minutes, then strain. Let cool before using.

From the top: Kashmiri Iced Tea,
Lychee Gimlet, Singapore Sling

Whiskey & Brandy Cocktails

Jujube Manhattan

WHISKEY AND BRANDY are the makings for handsome cocktails sipped by a fire during crisp fall or winter evenings but they perform equally well as summer refreshers when mixed with muddled fresh seasonal fruit, herbs or citrus. Very simply, the main difference between the two is that whiskey is distilled from fermented grain (a.k.a. beer) and brandy is distilled from fermented grape juice (a.k.a. wine), though fruits other than grapes are also sometimes used to make what's called "fruit brandy" (for the latter, usually the name of the fruit used is included on the label). The flavor of whiskey and brandy is greatly affected by the length of time spent aging—generally the longer the better.

Though brandies are made in many parts of the world, the most famous brandies come from Cognac and secondarily from Armagnac, two regions in southwestern France from which they take their name. Here is a quick lesson in deciphering some of the most common brandy labeling systems: A.C.=aged two years in wood; V.S. ("Very Special") or 3-Star=aged at least three years in wood; Napoleon=aged at least four years; V.S.O.P. ("Very Special Old Pale") or 5 Star=aged at least five years in wood; and Napoleon or Vieille Reserve or X.O. ("Extra or Extraordinary Old")=aged at least six years, although in particular X.O. is typically aged much longer.

While any brandy-based cocktail can be upgraded to Cognac, for the purpose of mixing, you need only a decent quality brandy (not the cheapest one on your liquor store's shelves but not an X.O. either).

Whiskey is produced in five countries, each of which produces a distinctly different style (or styles): Ireland (Irish Whiskey), Scotland (Scotch [single malt or blended whisky]), America (Bourbon, Tennessee Whiskey, Rye Whiskey, Blended American Whiskey), Canada (Canadian Whisky [blended]), and Japan ("Scotch" [single malt or blended]). The type of grain that is used and how it is processed, the method of distillation, and the aging method, and the method of blending all affect flavor. And just so you know, the spellings above aren't typos. American and Irish whiskey is spelled with an "e," but when referring to Scottish, Canadian and Japanese whisky, the "e" is dropped.

Here are some dos and don'ts for whiskey cocktails. When making a drink that calls for whiskey always use the type specified—in other words, don't substitute a blended whiskey for bourbon or scotch for rye. (There is one exception to this rule: bourbon can be used in place of rye whiskey as they are the most similar of all the whiskeys.) Single malt whisky should be used in a cocktail only when it's specifically called for. The complex and highly distinctive flavor of single malts make them very challenging to mix with other ingredients. We're lucky to boast two expertly mixed single-malt whisky cocktails—Stairway to Suntory and Milk and Honey.

Jujube manhattan

Though Manhattans are typically served up, this rustic version from Jujube looks great in a rocks glass. To be even more unorthodox, we like to serve this Manhattan with a spoon straw to fish out the delicious liquor soaked jujubes at the bottom of the glass. Maker's Mark bourbon is the ideal choice for this cocktail, but other bourbons will do just fine.

2 oz (60 ml) bourbon
2 tablespoons jujube "tea" or homemade jujube preserves
  (recipe follows)
2 dashes of orange bitters
¼ oz (7 ml) sweet vermouth
One maraschino cherry, for garnish

Combine the ingredients and enough ice to fill a rocks glass in a shaker. Shake vigorously and pour into a rocks glass. Add more ice if needed and garnish with the maraschino cherry.

HOMEMADE JUJUBE PRESERVES
15 large or 40 small dried jujubes
2 cups (500 ml) water
2 tablespoons honey
2½ tablespoons sugar

In a saucepan, combine 5 of the large jujubes or 12 of the small jujubes and the water and bring to a boil. Reduce the heat to medium and cook for 1 hour. While the jujubes are cooking, thinly slice the remaining jujubes. Some of the flesh will remain on the very small pits. As you work add the pits to the simmering water to extract their flavor. If your knife blade becomes sticky, run it under hot water. You should have about ½ cup (100 g) sliced jujubes. Over a bowl, strain the cooked jujubes in a fine-meshed sieve (or a colander lined with cheese cloth). Using a rubber spatula, crush the jujubes to extract their juice. Return the strained juice to the pan, add the honey and sugar and place over medium heat. Cook, stirring occasionally, for 5 to 7 minutes. Add the sliced jujubes and cook for 3 to 4 minutes. Remove from the heat and let cool completely before using. The syrup will thicken a little as it cools.

Stairway to suntory

In the last several years Japanese whiskeys have been gaining world attention, and taking home gold medals at international spirit competitions. The fruity-nutty flavor of Suntory's "Yamazaki" 12-year single malt whisky is a natural complement to orgeat—delicious almond-based syrup—and the apricot brandy used in this cocktail from the Lab Bar. You can use other single malt whiskies to make this drink—The Famous Grouse 12-year, Highland Park 12-year or Glenmorangie are all good options—but of course it's the Suntory that gives this cocktail its Asian twist.

½ oz (10 ml) orgeat or almond syrup
1 oz (30 ml) freshly squeezed lemon juice
Dash of egg white
½ oz plus ½ teaspoon (12.5 ml) apricot brandy
1¾ oz (52 ml) single malt whisky
Cinnamon stick, for garnish

Fill a rocks glass with ice. Combine the ingredients in an iced shaker and shake vigorously. Strain into the rocks glass. To prepare the garnish, toast the cinnamon stick with a lighter or match for 10 seconds all along its surface. Rub the rim of the glass with the stick and float it across the top of the cocktail.

Stairway
to Suntory

Milk and honey

Suntory's "Yamazaki" 12-year single malt whisky was the inspiration for this fantastic cocktail from Stanislav Vadra. The movie *Lost in Translation*, which centers around aging movie star Bob Harris (Bill Murray) who comes to Tokyo to promote Japanese whisky marketed by Suntory, brought Hollywood exposure to Japanese whisky, which, though lesser known in the West than scotch, is quickly gaining ground. In fact, Japan is the second-largest producer of single-malt whisky in the world after Scotland and has been producing whisky for nearly one hundred years. Other single malt whiskies can be used to make this drink—The Famous Grouse 12-year, Highland Park 12-year or Glenmorangie are all good options.

1 tablespoon plus 1 teaspoon (20 ml) hot milk
1 tablespoon plus 1 teaspoon (20 ml) honey
1 fresh or dried fig, plus a fig quarter for garnish
½ oz (15 ml) freshly squeezed lime juice
1¾ oz (52 ml) single malt whisky

Place the milk and honey in a mixing glass. Stir until the honey is dissolved. Add the fig. If you're using a dried fig, let the fig rest in the milk and honey for about 10 minutes to soften. Muddle the fig, then add ice, the lime juice and whisky. Shake vigorously and double strain into a chilled cocktail glass. Make a small slit in the middle of the fig quarter and place it on the rim of the glass.

From the top: Mikado, Shisho Smash

Mikado

This Japanese sounding cocktail, with not very Japanese ingredients, was named after an 1885 Gilbert and Sullivan operetta set in Japan. Crème de noyaux, a liqueur, has an almond flavor but is in fact made with various fruit pits—usually peach or apricot pits. (*Noyaux* means "fruit pits.") It is bright red and a just small amount will make a drink very red. This dry cocktail is not for imbibers with a sweet tooth.

1³/₄ oz (52 ml) brandy
¹/₂ teaspoon Cointreau
¹/₂ teaspoon orgeat or almond syrup
1 teaspoon crème de noyaux
Dash of Angostura bitters

Fill a rocks glass with ice. Combine the ingredients in an iced shaker and shake vigorously. Strain into the rocks glass.

Shisho smash

Rye is the whiskey of choice for this remake of the classic Whiskey Smash, though bourbon will also work. An American invention, rye whiskey is decidedly spicy and slightly bitter compared to bourbon, making it an ideal whiskey for cocktails where sweet ingredients like fruit juices or simple syrup balance its slight bitterness. The original Whiskey Smash calls for lemon and mint. Here yuzu juice and shiso give it an alluring Asian twist. If you don't have yuzu or shiso leaves on hand, you can make this drink with mint, plain simple syrup and lemon (be sure to increase amount of lemon if not using yuzu juice). It won't be Asian, but it will be a great drink!

1 lemon wedge (use 3 wedges if not using yuzu juice)
2 to 3 fresh shisho leaves torn into pieces or 4 to 6 fresh mint leaves
1 oz (30 ml) Shiso Syrup or Simple Syrup (page 21 or 19)
¹/₄ oz (7 ml) bottled yuzu juice (unsalted)
1³/₄ oz (52 ml) rye whiskey or bourbon
1 fresh shiso leaf or mint sprig, for garnish

Fill a rocks glass with crushed ice. Place the lemon wedge(s), shisho or mint leaves and Shisho Syrup or plain Simple Syrup in a glass mixing glass, and muddle. Add ice, the yuzu juice, if using, and whiskey. Shake vigorously and strain into the rocks glass. Garnish with a shisho leaf or sprig of mint and serve with a short straw.

Lychee alexander

This Asian twist on the Brandy Alexander is the perfect after-dinner treat and is hard to resist. We've included two versions: a classic recipe that calls for cream and a new-fangled version with ice cream that will require you to drag a blender out of your cupboard. Omit the brandy and lychee liqueur from No. 2 to create a delicious nonalcoholic treat.

NO. 1

1¼ oz (37 ml) brandy
¾ oz (22 ml) Lychee Syrup (page 21)
¼ oz (7 ml) lychee liqueur or an additional ¼ oz (7 ml) Lychee Syrup (page 21)
1 oz (30 ml) heavy cream
Chinese five spice powder, for garnish

Combine the ingredients in an iced shaker and shake vigorously. Strain into a chilled cocktail glass. Sprinkle a light dusting of Chinese five spice powder over top.

NO. 2

1½ oz (45 ml) brandy
2 lychees
¼ oz (7 ml) lychee liqueur or liquid from lychee can
2 large scoops vanilla ice cream
Chinese five spice powder, for garnish

Place the ingredients in a blender. Process until smooth. Pour into a chilled cocktail glass. Sprinkle a light dusting of Chinese five spice powder over top.

The Dragonfly

The dragonfly

Make this pretty cocktail from Jujube in summer when watermelons are full of flavor. Maker's Mark is a good choice for this cocktail, but any bourbon will do.

Seven 1-inch (2.5-cm) chunks of fresh, seedless watermelon
5 fresh Thai basil leaves
1 oz (30 ml) Simple Syrup (page 19)
¼ oz (7 ml) freshly squeezed lime juice
1½ oz (45 ml) bourbon
Lime wedge or watermelon cubes, for garnish

Puree the watermelon chunks in a blender. You should have about 4 ounces (125 ml) of puree. Set aside. Place the Thai basil leaves and 2 ice cubes in mixing glass and muddle. Add a generous amount of ice, the Simple Syrup, lime juice, watermelon puree and bourbon. Shake vigorously and pour into a pint glass. Add more ice if needed and garnish with a lime wedge or spear of watermelon cubes.

Lychee Alexander

Japanese cocktail

This is possibly the oldest Asian-inspired cocktail around. It dates back to at least 1862, when it made its first appearance in the 1862 edition of Jerry Thomas's famous bar book *How to Mix Drinks*. David Wondrich, author of *Imbibe*, speculates that Thomas created the drink in 1860 to commemorate the first Japanese legation to the United States, members of which likely visited Thomas's bar. Of course there's nothing really Asian about it, but this simple yet elegant cocktail is reason plenty to stock your bar with some orgeat syrup.

1 piece lemon peel
2 oz (60 ml) brandy
$\frac{1}{2}$ oz (15 ml) orgeat or almond syrup
2 dashes of Angostura bitters
Lemon twist, for garnish

Place the lemon peel in a mixing glass and muddle. Add ice and the rest of the ingredients. Stir thoroughly and strain into a chilled cocktail glass. Garnish with the lemon twist.

Oriental cocktail

This refreshing whiskey cocktail has a nice balance of sweet and sour, and a good story. According to the writer of *The Savoy Cocktail Book* (1930), an American engineer fell desperately ill with fever while in the Philippines. He survived due to the extraordinary care given to him by a doctor, to whom he gave this cocktail recipe as a way of showing his gratitude. Though the recipes that have come down to us call for lime juice, the dear doctor would have likely used the native Filipino citrus called calamansi—thus our revisionist version. Both versions are equally delicious.

$1\frac{1}{2}$ oz (45 ml) rye whiskey or bourbon
$\frac{3}{4}$ oz (22 ml) sweet vermouth
$\frac{3}{4}$ oz (22 ml) triple sec
$\frac{1}{2}$ oz plus $\frac{3}{4}$ teaspoon (20 ml) defrosted frozen or freshly squeezed calamansi juice or $\frac{1}{2}$ oz (15 ml) freshly squeezed lime juice

Combine all the ingredients in an iced shaker and shake vigorously. Strain into a chilled cocktail glass.

The hot date

This cocktail from Jujube perfectly combines sweet, sour and spicy taste sensations—making it hard to resist. The big bourbon flavor of Jim Beam, the bourbon of choice for this cocktail, is a good match for the spicy cayenne pepper.

$1\frac{3}{4}$ oz (52 ml) bourbon
$\frac{1}{2}$ oz (15 ml) freshly squeezed lemon juice
Dash of ground red pepper (cayenne)
2 tablespoons jujube "tea" or Homemade Jujube Preserves (page 66)
One maraschino cherry, for garnish

Combine the ingredients and enough ice to fill a rocks glass in a shaker. Shake vigorously and pour into a rocks glass. Add more ice if needed and garnish with the maraschino cherry.

whiskey & brandy cocktails

From left to right: Japanese Cocktail, Oriental Cocktail

Sake, Wine &
Champagne Cocktails

Green Tea Cocktail

LOOKING FOR THE PERFECT APERITIF or an afternoon refresher? Cocktails made with wine, champagne or sake are the answer.

All of the major categories of wine are featured in this chapter: still (Sake Sangria), fortified (the Bamboo Cocktail), and sparkling, of which champagne is the most famous example (too many to mention). While Japanese plum wine is not technically a fortified wine, it is usually a little higher in alcohol content than table wine and does has sherrylike qualities. It is used in several drinks, including the Tokyo Manhattan, Plum Wine Cobbler and our pitcher-size Sake Sangria.

Champagne, the granddaddy of sparkling wines, uses the *méthode Champenoise*, which means that the wine undergoes its fizz-producing second fermentation in the same bottle in which it will be sold. Though only true champagne comes from Champagne, sparkling wine producers from other regions in France and other parts of the world may use the traditional *méthode Champenoise*, creating wines that have similar qualities as champagne. (Look for "traditional method" or *méthode Champenoise* on the label.) The increasingly popular and affordably priced Italian sparkling wine known as Prosecco is used in the famous Bellini and in our Asian version— the Asian Pear Bellini. Sparkling wines made in the traditional method can range from very dry to very sweet, but for cocktails the best choice is generally brut (the driest), extra dry (less dry) or sec (semidry). Prosecco is generally lighter and more fruity than champagne. Remember that sparkling wines will lose their fizz once opened, so either plan to make several champagne cocktails in the same evening or to enjoy some of the bubbly straight up (so much pressure, I know).

Though often referred to as "rice wine" in English because of its winelike qualities, sake is made from fermented rice instead of fruit. There are four basic grades of sake, each of which requires different brewing methods and a different amount of rice milling: junmai, honjozo, ginjo and daiginjo. A fifth designation is namazake, which means unpasteurized and can be applied to all four grades. The best type of sakes to use in cocktails are junmai, ginjo and junmai-ginjo. Junmai is pure rice wine with no distilled alcohol added to it. It is slightly more acidic than the other sakes, which enables it to blend with a wide range of flavors. Ginjo requires more milling than junmai and has a little alcohol added to it. Its flavor is quite subtle and tends to be slightly softer than Junmai. If you see the label "Junmai Ginjo" that means no alcohol has been added. Momokawa's "Diamond" junmai ginjo, Gekkeikan's "Traditional" sake, which is a junmai, Masumi Okuden Kantsukuri's "Mirror of Truth" junmai, Dewazakura's Dewasansan "Green Ridge" junmai ginjo, and Shirayuki's junmai or junmai ginjo are some popular sake choices for cocktails.

Green tea cocktail

This striking champagne cocktail has a beautifully eerie and glowing green color. With its flavors in perfect balance, both green tea and champagne fans will find something to love in this cocktail.

1 oz (30 ml) Zen Green Tea Liqueur
5 oz (150 ml) chilled champagne
Twist of lemon

Place the green tea liqueur in a mixing glass with a handful of ice. Stir briefly to chill. Strain into a champagne flute. Add the champagne. Rub the lemon twist around the rim of the glass and drop into the cocktail.

White light tini

This cocktail from Pure Food and Wine is named for the inner white light that floods through the external mind or third eye of an enlightened being. In keeping with the emphasis on the use of organic and unprocessed ingredients, the folks at Pure Food and Wine like to use unfiltered (nigori) sake and agave to sweeten the spicy ginger juice. Nigori sake is relatively sweet and has a cloudy white appearance. It should be shaken before being used. This light cocktail is garnished with an edible flower, which are once again in vogue and have a new home in the cocktail where they add flavor and beauty. A note to the wise when using flowers to garnish cocktails: Not all flowers are edible (some are poisonous!), so check resources online or books on the subject for guidance before eating them. And only eat or pick organically grown flowers that are pesticide-free.

¾ teaspoon strained ginger juice derived from one 1-in (2.5-cm) chunk ginger root (see page 15)
1½ oz (45 ml) chilled Lemongrass Green Tea (recipe follows)
1½ oz (45 ml) sake
¼ oz (7 ml) freshly squeezed lime juice
½ oz (15 ml) agave nectar or ¾ oz (22 ml) Simple Syrup (page 19)
Edible white flower, such as a nasturtium, for garnish (optional)

Combine the ingredients in an iced shaker and shake vigorously. Strain into a chilled cocktail glass. Garnish with the edible white flower, if using.

LEMONGRASS GREEN TEA
Makes 1 cup (250 ml)
1 stalk fresh lemongrass
2 teaspoons jasmine green tea or 1 teaspoon each jasmine green tea and snow dragon green tea
1 cup (250 ml) water

Wash the lemongrass and cut about ½ inch (1.25 cm) off the hard root ends and the top one-third off the stalks, and discard. Remove the tough outer layers and discard. Bruise the tender white stalk with the broad side of a chef's knife. Chop the stalk and combine it with the tea in a cup. Heat the water until it barely begins to simmer (do not let it come to a boil). Pour the heated water into the cup. Steep the tea for 2 to 3 minutes. Strain the tea and let cool before using.

NOTE: Agave nectar is made from a sticky juice derived from the agave plant (not the same variety of agave used to make tequila). It hit the U.S. health food industry in the last decade and has now found its way into alcoholic beverages—as part of the niche trend of healthy or organic cocktails. It's considered a healthy sweetener due to its low glycemic level.

Rising sun

Crisp, tart and slightly vegetal, gooseberries are ideal for this cocktail from Ariana Johnson of Modus Club, though raspberries or blackberries are very good substitutes. If you're using brut or extra champagne, use 3 teaspoons sugar. This elegant cocktail makes a great aperitif and goes great with nuts or a mild cheese. Wokka Saki has an alcohol content similar to vodka, so keep that in mind when imbibing. With a name like Wokka Saki how could we not include this cocktail with our favorite sake-based cocktails?

5 to 6 gooseberries, raspberries or blackberries, plus 1 for garnish
2 to 3 teaspoons sugar
1 oz (30 ml) Wokka Saki or vodka plus a splash of sake
Chilled prosecco or champagne, for topping

If you're using gooseberries, remove them from their leaves. Combine the gooseberries or other berries and sugar in a mixing glass and muddle. Add enough ice to fill a rocks glass and the Wokka Saki. Shake vigorously and pour into a rocks glass. Add more ice if needed. Top with the prosecco or champagne. Garnish with a gooseberry in its leaf or a raspberry or blackberry.

Left to right: Dream On, Pomegranate Royale

Dream on

This subtle cocktail from Stanislav Vadrna is flavorful yet light. It's the perfect aperitif—something to appreciate before your taste buds have enjoyed bolder main course flavors. And if you're looking for something to do with the extra sage you bought for Thanksgiving dinner, you've found it. Stan prefers Bombay gin for this cocktail but other gins such Tanqueray or Gordon's will also work. Beefeater, however, is too aromatic.

3 chunks fresh pineapple
2 fresh sage leaves
1¼ oz (37 ml) schochu
¾ oz (22) ml gin
2 teaspoons (10 ml) Grand Marnier
About 1¾ oz (50 ml) brut champagne, preferably Moet Chandon

Place the pineapple and sage in a mixing glass and muddle. Add ice, the shochu, gin and Grand Marnier. Shake vigorously and double strain into a chilled large champagne flute. Top with the champagne.

Pomegranate royale

When sipping on this pomegranate-colored cocktail from Jujube, it's easy to imagine yourself seated at a leather banquette in a wood-paneled lounge with brass fittings. It's that classy. If you like a dry cocktail, use brut champagne. If you like a sweeter touch, use a demi-sec champagne or cava (or other moderately sweet sparkling wine).

1 oz (30 ml) Pomegranate-Ginger Syrup (page 21)
About 4 oz (120 ml) chilled sparkling wine

Pour the Pomegranate-Ginger syrup into a chilled champagne flute. Top with the sparkling wine.

Sake mojito

This ultralight version of the Latin classic from Pod is the perfect refresher on a hot summer day. The folks at Pod like to use Shirayuki sake for this cocktail.

10 to 12 fresh mint leaves
½ oz (15 ml) Simple Syrup (page 19)
¼ oz (7 ml) freshly squeezed lime juice
2 oz (60 ml) sake
Club soda, for topping
Lime wedge, for garnish

Place the mint leaves, Simple Syrup and fresh lime juice in a mixing glass and muddle. Add enough ice to fill a highball glass and the sake and shake. Pour into a highball glass and add more ice if needed. Top with the club soda and stir briefly. Garnish with the lime wedge.

Bamboo cocktail

Invented by Louis Eppinger in the 1890s, the manager of the Grand Hotel in Yokohama, Japan, this cocktail—a most perfect aperatif—will transport you to a turn-of-the-last-century gentle elegance when sherry was king. Most recipes for the Bamboo Cocktail specify dry sherry or simply sherry. But this cocktail is exceedingly better when made with a medium-dry amontillado sherry rather than a very dry (fino) sherry. Amontillado is a amber-colored medium-dry variety of sherry that is darker than fino but lighter than the sweeter oloroso sherries. Sandeman Character Amontillado is a good choice. (Thanks to David Wondrich for this recommendation.)

1½ oz (45 ml) medium-dry sherry
1½ oz (45 ml) dry vermouth
2 dashes of orange bitters
2 dashes of Angostura bitters
Lemon twist, for garnish

Combine the ingredients in an iced mixing glass. Stir thoroughly and strain into a chilled cocktail glass. Garnish with the lemon twist.

Heavenly gates

Named after a mahjong hand, this subtle champagne cocktail from Miguel Aranda is a lovely aperitif or accompaniment to brunch. The delicious Lychee Puree is used in two nonalcoholic cocktails in the next chapter.

1 oz (30 ml) Lychee Puree (recipe follows)
½ oz (15 ml) gin
About 2 oz (60 ml) chilled sparkling wine
1 lychee, for garnish (optional)

In an iced shaker, combine the Lychee Puree and gin. Shake vigorously and strain into a chilled champagne flute. Top with the sparkling wine. Garnish with the lychee, if using.

LYCHEE PUREE
Makes 2 cups (500 ml)
One 20-oz (565-g) can lychees in syrup
½ cup (125 ml) freshly squeezed lemon juice
½ cup (125 g) sugar

Blend the lychees and their syrup with the lemon juice and sugar in a food processor or blender. Strain the liquid and place in a clean jar. Leftover puree will keep for 1 week in the refrigerator.

Bamboo Cocktail

From left: Little Tokyo Cooler, Tokyo Manhattan

Tokyo manhattan

This cocktail, adapted from Junior Portal's of Betty's Wok & Noodle, will appeal to those who like their manhattans on the sweet rather than dry side. We added orange bitters to the mix, because even a sake Manhattan deserves a touch 'o bitters.

3 oz (90 ml) sake
1½ oz (45 ml) Japanese plum wine
3 to 4 dashes of orange bitters
One maraschino cherry, for garnish

Combine the ingredients in an iced mixing glass. Stir thoroughly. Strain into a chilled cocktail glass and drop in the cherry.

Little tokyo cooler

Despite a touch of sweetness from cane syrup (a top shelf sweetener), the overall effect of this drink from Timothy Lacey of Spring is one of dry, crystal clear elegance. The aroma of cool cucumber and the delicate flavor of peppery-tart pink pepper make this a very enticing drink, and a perfect aperitif. Citric acid, available at health food stores, adds a pleasant tartness to the mix.

1½ tablespoons peeled and chopped Japanese, "baby," or English cucumber
1 teaspoon whole pink peppercorns or whole green peppercorns
Pinch of sea salt or kosher salt
2 pinches of citric acid
2 teaspoons cane syrup or 2:1 Simple Syrup (page 19)
2 oz (60 ml) Wokka Saki or vodka plus a splash of sake
Splash of club soda

Fill a rocks glass with ice. Combine the cucumber, peppercorns, salt, citric acid and cane syrup in a mixing glass or cocktail shaker and muddle. Add ice and the Wokka Saki and stir thoroughly. Double strain into the rocks glass. Top with the club soda and stir briefly.

NOTE: Wokka Saki is a unique blend of vodka, sake and natural flavors that has an alcohol content similar to vodka. Keep the higher alcohol content of this spirit in mind when imbibing.

Kyoto colada

This fun cocktail from Junior Portal of Betty's Wok & Noodle is a perfect blend of east and west. To create a virgin Kyota Colada, simply omit the sake.

4 oz (125 ml) sake
1¾ oz (52 ml) pineapple juice
1¾ oz (52 ml) coconut syrup
Splash of heavy cream
½ an orange wheel, for garnish

Combine the ingredients in a blender with enough ice to fill a pint glass and blend until frothy. Pour into a chilled pint glass and garnish with the orange wheel.

Sake rojito

This is another great sake creation from Junior Portal of Betty's Wok & Noodle, named for the slight rose color of cranberry juice and plum wine.

3 teaspoons sugar
3 lime wedges
1 oz (30 ml) freshly squeezed lime juice
3 oz (90 ml) sake
3 oz (90 ml) Japanese plum wine
Splash of cranberry juice

Place the sugar and lime wedges in a mixing glass and muddle. Add ice and the rest of the ingredients. Shake vigorously and pour into a pint glass. Add more ice if needed.

Kyoto Colada

Watermelon smash

Pretty in pink, this uncomplicated cocktail from Miguel Aranda combines spicy ginger and sweet citrus for a refreshing summer smash. Watermelon plays a starring role in this drink, so be sure to use summer melons at the height of their flavor.

½ cup (125 g) watermelon cubes
3 to 4 slices peeled fresh ginger
½ oz (15 ml) sweetened calamansi concentrate or other sweetened lime juice or ¼ oz (7 ml) each defrosted frozen or freshly squeezed calamansi juice and Simple Syrup (page 19)
1¾ oz (52 ml) Wokka Saki or vodka plus a splash of sake
1 thin wedge of watermelon (with rind), for garnish
Sliced crystallized ginger candy, for garnish

Combine the watermelon cubes, ginger slices and sweetened calamansi or lime in a mixing glass and muddle. Add enough ice to fill a rocks glass and the Wokka Saki and shake vigorously. Pour into a rocks glass. To garnish, cut a short slice into the flesh of the watermelon wedge and balance it on the rim of the glass. Slide a few pieces of candied ginger onto a cocktail pick and spear the rind of the watermelon.

Clockwise from top: Asian Sour, Honeydew
Drop, Loca-motion, Grand Pagoda

Asian sour

This cocktail, adapted from Kubo Radio, is a spin on an Amaretto Sour. Spicy fresh pear ginger juice is a wonderful complement to the Amaretto and pear liquor.

2 oz (60 ml) sake
$1/_4$ oz (7 ml) pear liqueur
$1/_4$ oz (7 ml) amaretto
$1/_2$ oz (15 ml) freshly squeezed lime juice
$3^1/_2$ oz (120 ml) pear juice
1 teaspoon strained ginger juice derived from one $1^1/_4$-in
　(3-cm) piece fresh ginger (see page 15)
Lime wheel, for garnish

Combine the ingredients in an iced shaker and shake vigorously. Strain into a chilled cocktail glass and garnish with the lime wheel.

Loca-motion

Accessorized with a sparkling pink rim, this fruity, tropical cocktail from Junior Portal of Betty's Wok & Noodle combines Asian and Latin ingredients with style.

Sugar and grenadine (see page 21), for rimming
4 oz (125 ml) sake
$3/_4$ oz (22 ml) coconut syrup
$1^1/_4$ oz (37 ml) passion fruit juice or 2 tablespoons fresh
　passion fruit pulp (from 1 passion fruit)
Splash of freshly squeezed lime juice

Place a small amount of grenadine in a saucer, and a small amount of sugar in another saucer. Lightly dip a large chilled cocktail glass into the grenadine (apply just a whisper of grenadine to the rim—just enough to lightly color the rim and give a base for the sugar to adhere to). Then dip the glass in the sugar.

　Combine the ingredients in an iced shaker and shake vigorously. Strain into the rimmed glass. If you're using fresh passion fruit pulp, double strain the cocktail.

Grand pagoda

With its rouge tint and white coconut topping, this slightly sweet drink from Kubu Radio is like a gift-wrapped present—perfect after dinner or when you want to indulge in something pretty and pink.

$1^1/_2$ oz (45 ml) sake
$1/_2$ oz (15 ml) crème de cassis
$1/_4$ oz (7 ml) freshly squeezed lime juice
$2^1/_2$ oz (75 ml) pineapple juice
Dried coconut shavings, for garnish
One maraschino cherry, for garnish

Combine the ingredients in an iced shaker and shake vigorously. Strain into a chilled cocktail glass and sprinkle coconut shavings across the top of the cocktail (the top of the cocktail should be nice and frothy for the coconut shavings to sit on). Drop in the maraschino cherry.

Asian pear bellini

The classic Bellini, a favorite brunch cocktail, is made with white peach puree. This version from Buddakan is made with Asian pear and is dressed up with a Sugar and Five Spice Rimmer.

Sugar and Five Spice, to rim glass (recipe follows)
2 tablespoons chilled Asian Pear Puree (recipe follows)
3 oz (90 ml) chilled prosecco

Rim a chilled champagne flute with the Sugar and Five Spice Rimmer. Add the Asian Pear Puree, then slowly add the prosecco, stirring constantly to combine the ingredients.

SUGAR AND FIVE SPICE RIMMER
Makes about 1/2 cup (125 g)
1/2 cup (125 g) sugar
1 tablespoon ground cinnamon
Pinch of Chinese five spice powder

Combine the ingredients in a flat, shallow saucer and mix well before rimming the glass. Store any leftover in an airtight container.

ASIAN PEAR PUREE
Makes about 1/2 cup (125 ml)
1 Asian pear, cored and coarsely chopped (leave peel on)
2 tablespoons sugar
3/4 cup (200 ml) water
1/2 teaspoon freshly squeezed lemon juice

Place the chopped pear, sugar and water in a medium saucepan and gently simmer over medium heat until the pear is soft. Strain the pear and set aside to cool. Puree the pear and lemon juice in a blender or food processor. Leftover puree will keep for 3 or 4 days in the refrigerator.

Honeydew drop

The balance of sweet and sour with exotic undertones of lemongrass and kaffir lime leaves is intoxicating in this cocktail from Stanislav Vadra. Licor 43, a Spanish liqueur, provides a subtle flavor of vanilla and citrus, making this cocktail a true East-West creation. This is the ideal cocktail to serve when you want to impress someone with a drink that's lightly alcoholic yet full of body and flavor.

1 slice honeydew melon, cut into chunks
1/2 oz (15 ml) freshly squeezed lime juice
1/2 oz (15 ml) Lemongrass and Kaffir Leaf Syrup (page 20)
2 teaspoons (10 ml) Licor 43
1 3/4 oz (52 ml) sake
One fresh or dried Kaffir lime leaf, left whole or slivered, for garnish

Place the melon and the lime juice in a mixing glass and muddle. Add ice and the rest of the ingredients and shake vigorously. Double strain into a chilled cocktail glass. Float the lime leaf on the top of the cocktail.

Asian Pear Belini

Zen phizz

In this light and refreshing cocktail from Monsoon sparking wine and delicious fruit flavor are harmoniously combined.

1½ oz (45 ml) peach schnapps
1 oz (30 ml) mango juice
Sparkling wine

Fill a collins glass with ice. Combine the peach schnapps and the mango juice in an iced shaker and shake vigorously. Strain into the glass, top with sparkling wine and stir. Garnish with a slice of fresh ripe mango.

From the top: Zen Phizz, Plum Wine Cobbler, Sake Sangria

Plum wine cobbler

The original cobbler was made with sherry, and with its sherrylike qualities, plum wine pays homage to Western and Eastern traditions simultaneously. Shiso and umeboshi (plum) are a favorite combination in Japan. If you enjoy the taste of shiso, make a variant of this cobbler by using $1/4$ ounce (7 ml) each of Simple Syrup and Shiso Syrup (pages 19 and 21).

3 tangerine slices or 2 orange slices
$1/2$ oz (15 ml) Simple Syrup (page 19)
4 oz (125 ml) Japanese plum wine
2 to 3 plum slices, for garnish

Fill a collins glass with crushed ice. Place the orange or tangerine slices and Simple Syrup in a mixing glass and muddle lightly. Add ice and the Japanese plum wine and shake vigorously. Strain into the ice-filled collins glass. Make small slits into the flesh of the plum slices and place them on the rim of the glass. Serve with a straw.

NOTE: Like plum wine, Chinese rice wine (Shaoxing), or "yellow wine," has sherrylike qualities and makes an excellent cobbler. However, it's more difficult to find good drinking-quality Shaoxing than plum wine. If you can lay your hands on some, you can make Rice Wine Cobbler by replacing the plum wine with rice wine and changing the garnish to an orange slice. Look for Shaoxing wine that has been aged at least five years and preferably ten years. Do not use the type meant for cooking that is available at grocery stores (and has salt added).

Sake sangria

In Japan "san" is appended to people names to show polite deference and honor. This subtle yet flavorful version of the classic fruity and often fortified wine drink could easily be called Gria-san, in deference to its wondrous plenitude. Since the best Sangria should be allowed to rest for at least an hour, if not overnight, we've made this recipe a pitcher-size quantity—if you're going to go to the trouble . . .

Makes about six 6-ounce (175-ml) servings
$1/2$ Asian pear, thinly sliced
$1/2$ fugi apple, thinly sliced
2 plums, thinly sliced
$1/2$ cup (125 ml) tangerine or orange juice
$1^1/2$ cups (375 ml) sake
$1^1/2$ cups (375 ml) light fruity white wine (such as Pinot Grigio)
1 cup (250 ml) Japanese plum wine

Place the fruit slices and tangerine juice in the bottom of a large glass or ceramic pitcher. Lightly muddle the fruit. Add the rest of the ingredients and stir. Refrigerate for at least one hour or overnight. Serve in white wine glasses.

Nonalcoholic Drinks & Bar Snacks

Lychee Colada

"FOOD IS THE CURSE OF THE DRINKING CLASSES," wrote British novelist and avid drinker Kingsley Amis. We love Kingsley, and his books on drinking are highly entertaining, but on this point we have to disagree. We think every tipple deserves a nibble.

To help you keep your guests (or yourself) from fading too early in the evening, we've included eight bar snacks. Edamame and Wakame Chips—two of the simplest to prepare—are common bar snacks in Asia. Others are Asian riffs on favorite snacks in the West—Curry Popcorn, Tamari Almonds and Deviled Eggs Asian Style. Sweet Yam Fries with Spicy Soy Dipping Sauce or Grilled Satays offer even greater sustenance, making that late night call for pizza delivery less likely. Even if you don't feel like making any of the bar snacks in this chapter we recommend that you have some of your favorite noshing foods available to guests when cocktails are being served.

When everyone at your party has received something muddled, shaken and strained, it's nice to be able to offer your handful of abstaining guests something equally delicious, equally special and equally handcrafted as the finest cocktail. By comparison opening a nonalcoholic beer or pouring some seltzer in a glass will seem anticlimactic to both you and your guests. What's the fun of that? We've provided ten

hooch-free cocktails in this chapter for just this instance, or for when you're simply in the mood for a refreshing drink anytime of the day or for any occasion. Similarly to the cocktails in the other chapters, these recipes range in number of ingredients and techniques. Some, like Vietnamese Lime Soda and Iced Chrysanthemum Tea, are simpler to prepare than a Shirley Temple; others require techniques like muddling, or the preparation of the well-utilized Lychee Puree, or even making hot chocolate to be cooled and then used in the Chocolate Cocktail (but, oh, is it worth it).

When serving cocktails or snacks we always like to have ice-cold pitchers of fresh water on hand. On occasion we infuse water with fruits, herb and aromatics (and even the cool cucumber)—it's extremely easy to do and immediately ratchets up the "special" factor of parties. Ingredients are infused in a pitcher of water for a few hours in the refrigerator, and ice is added just before serving. Here are a few suggestions, although you can use whatever fresh ingredients you have on hand and combinations you are willing to try: Cucumber wheels or sliced kiwi and mint leaves; fresh pineapple chunks or lychees and sliced fresh ginger root; fresh lemongrass stalks, trimmed, peeled and bruised; Sprigs of Thai basil; dried hibiscus or jasmine leaves.

Green-teani

With bit of caffeine in the green tea, this delicious nonalcoholic cocktail offers a different sort of buzz.

3 oz (90 ml) chilled Green Tea (see recipe below)
1½ oz (45 ml) Lychee Puree (page 80)
1 lychee (optional)

Combine the green tea and Lychee Puree in an iced shaker and shake vigorously. Strain into a chilled cocktail glass. Drop the lychee, if using, into the drink for a surprise sweet treat.

GREEN TEA
Makes 1 cup (250 ml)
1 teaspoon loose-leaf green tea or 1 bag green tea
1 cup (250 ml) water

Place the tea in a cup. Heat the water until it barely begins to simmer (do not let it come to a boil). Pour the heated water in the cup. Steep the tea for 2 to 3 minutes. Strain the tea and let cool before using.

Chocolate cocktail

This luxurious, intensely chocolatey drink leaves one wanting for naught—which isn't always the case when imbibing in a "mocktail." The texture of the chocolate becomes smoother as it cools down and becomes quite velvety if left to chill overnight before using. Because simple syrup, which is half water, sweetens the chocolate and the chilled chocolate is shook with ice before serving, it's important to use whole milk. We don't recommend using a 2 percent or low-fat milk. If you want an even richer drink, experiment with using some half-and-half or cream. This cocktail can be served up in a cocktail glass or, if you're in the mood for something more casual, over ice in a highball glass. The chilled chocolate can be kept in the refrigerator for up to a week.

Makes 3 chocolate martinis or iced chocolate highballs
1¼ cups (300 ml) whole milk
5 oz (150 g) bittersweet chocolate pistoles, chips or finely
  chopped off a block
5 to 6 tablespoons Spicy Thai Basil Syrup (page 21)
¼ teaspoon pure vanilla extract
Pinch of kosher salt or sea salt
6 to 8 fresh Thai basil leaves, for muddling (per cocktail)
Cocao powder or sprigs of Thai basil, for garnish

In a small saucepan, add the milk and bring to a simmer over low heat. Whisk in the chocolate until completely melted. Whisk in the Spicy Thai Basil Simple Syrup, vanilla extract and salt. Remove from the heat and let

cool completely before using or place in the refrigerator to chill overnight. If chilled overnight, stir until smooth before using. To make one chocolate martini, dust the rim of a chilled cocktail glass with cocao powder.

To make an iced chocolate drink, fill a highball glass with ice. Place the Thai basil leaves and a couple of cubes of ice in a mixing glass. Muddle the basil leaves. Add 4½ oz (140 ml) of the chilled chocolate to the glass and fill with ice. Shake vigorously and strain into the rimmed cocktail glass or the ice-filled highball glass. Garnish the iced chocolate drink with a sprig of mint. Repeat with the remainder of the chilled chocolate or reserve for later use.

Lychee colada

This virgin colada with an Asian twist is a pleasantly fruity cocktail—perfect for those who eschew rum. If you're using canned pineapple juice for this cocktail, be sure to shake it thoroughly before opening. This cocktail was inspired by a lychee colada from Pure Food and Wine in New York City. Cream of coconut is presweetened and is often found on the same shelf with other cocktail supplies.

1³⁄₄ oz (52 ml) pineapple juice
¹⁄₂ oz (15 ml) freshly squeezed orange juice
1 teaspoon cream of coconut
³⁄₄ oz (22 ml) lychee juice
2 to 3 small pieces fresh pineapple, for garnish (optional)

Combine the ingredients in an iced shaker and shake vigorously. Strain into a chilled cocktail glass. Place 2 or 3 small pieces of pineapple, if using, on a cocktail spear and place in the glass.

From left to right: Chocolate Cocktail, Green-teani

Clockwise from the top: Peach and Passion Fruit Smash, Lychee Lemon Soda, Pineapple Refresher

Peach & passion fruit smash

This delicious combination of peaches and passion fruit is adapted from a cocktail included in a *New York Times* recipe round-up on the trend of new and better "grown-up" nonalcoholic cocktails. Our adaptation gave us a way to work in the delicious Ginger Syrup from Lantern, which we can't get enough of. This cocktail is best when made with fresh in-season peaches.

½ fresh peach, peeled and sliced, or 6 defrosted frozen peach slices
5 to 6 fresh mint leaves, plus 1 mint sprig for garnish
2 tablespoons fresh passion fruit pulp or 1 oz (30 ml) bottled passion fruit juice
1 oz (30 ml) Ginger Syrup (page 19)
¼ oz (7 ml) freshly squeezed lime juice (increase to ½ oz or 15 ml if using bottled passion fruit juice)
Club soda, to top

Place the peach slices and mint leaves in a mixing glass and muddle until the peaches have released their juice. Add enough ice to fill a Collins glass and the remainder of the ingredients, except the club soda. Shake vigorously and pour into a collins glass. Top with the club soda and stir briefly. Garnish with the mint sprig.

Lychee lemon soda

This summer quaff was inspired by the delicious Lychee Puree from mixologist Miguel Aranda. We just had to find another use for it! It's that good.

8 to 10 fresh mint leaves
1 teaspoon sugar
¼ oz (7 ml) freshly squeezed lemon juice
3½ oz (100 ml) Lychee Puree (page 80)
1 oz (30 ml) water
Club soda, to top
Mint sprig, for garnish

Place the mint leaves, sugar and lemon juice in a mixing glass and muddle. Add enough ice to fill a large collins glass and the remainder of the ingredients, except the club soda. Shake vigorously and pour into a large collins glass. Add more ice if needed. Top with the club soda and stir briefly. Garnish with the mint sprig.

Pineapple refresher

Calpico, the base of this thirst-quenching drink from Morimoto, is a ready-to-drink Japanese beverage made from nonfat milk. It has a light, sweet, tangy flavor and can be mixed with any variety of fruit juice for a healthy and refreshing drink.

Two 1-in (2.5-cm) chunks fresh pineapple
4 oz (125 ml) Calpico
3 oz (90 ml) pineapple juice
3 to 4 fresh coriander (cilantro) leaves, torn
Pineapple wedge, for garnish

Place the pineapple in mixing glass and muddle until the fruit has released its juice. Add enough ice to fill a collins glass and the remainder of the ingredients. Shake vigorously and pour into a collins glass. Add more ice if needed. Garnish with the pineapple wedge.

Vietnamese lime soda

Vietnamese restaurants usually serve a wide variety of refreshing homemade sodas, called *chanh*. This recipe can also be made with fresh lemon juice. Salty drinks are very common in tropical climes where they help to cool and replenish the body.

1 oz (30 ml) freshly squeezed lime juice
½ oz (15 ml) Simple Syrup (page 19)
Pinch of kosher salt or sea salt
Club soda, for topping
Lime wheel, for garnish

Fill a highball glass with ice. Combine the lime juice, Simple Syrup and salt in an iced shaker and shake vigorously. Strain into the iced highball glass. Top with the club soda and stir briefly. Garnish with the lime wheel.

Tamarind cooler

Tamarind has an intense sweet-sour flavor that is used widely in Indian and Southeast Asian seasoning pastes and sauces. Easy-to-use tamarind concentrate is now available in many supermarkets.

½ cup (125 ml) boiling hot water
1½ teaspoons tamarind concentrate (see page 17)
2 teaspoons minced crystallized ginger candy
2 teaspoons freshly squeezed lemon juice
¾ oz (22 ml) Simple Syrup (page 19)
Club soda, for topping
Lemon wheel, for garnish

Combine the boiling hot water, tamarind and minced crystallized ginger candy in a small heatproof bowl and whisk until the tamarind is completely dissolved. Set aside to steep for 30 minutes. Fill a highball glass with crushed ice. Strain the steeped mixture into a mixing glass. Add ice, the lemon juice and Simple Syrup and shake vigorously. Strain into the ice-filled highball glass. Top with the club soda and stir briefly. Garnish with the lemon wheel.

Iced chrysanthemum tea

Chrysanthemum is used in traditional Chinese medicine for its cooling and detoxifying properties. In Japan, they're used fresh in stir-fries and salad dressing. You can omit the simple syrup if you prefer the tangy, slightly bitter flavor of pure chrysanthemum.

Makes two 8-ounce (250-ml) servings
5 whole, dried chrysanthemum flowers
2 cups (500 ml) water
1 oz (30 ml) Simple Syrup (page 19) (optional)

Rinse the dried chrysanthemum and combine them with the water in a pan. Bring to a boil, reduce the heat and simmer for 20 minutes. Remove from heat and strain, reserving the steeped flowers for garnish. Combine the tea with the Simple Syrup and chill. When ready to serve, fill two collins or ice tea glasses with ice. Pour the tea into the glasses and float a steeped chrysanthemum flower in each glass.

Counterclockwise from the top:
Vietnamese Lime Soda, Tamarind
Cooler, Iced Chrysanthemum Tea

Wakame chips

Korean cookbook authors Deborah Samuels and Taekyung Chung shared this simple snack recipe with us. These small seaweed chips come preseasoned with the natural saltiness of sea water. The saltiness may be intense for some, so we suggest offering a companion snack that is less salty or slightly sweet for contrast—such as Deviled Eggs or Oven-dried Pineapple. Wakame comes preshredded in packages. Ito wakame—the Korean variety—comes in long thin pieces, which allows you to cut the wakame to custom chip sizes. Ito wakame is available at Korean grocers or specialty Asian grocers.

Makes ¾ cup (60 g)
1 tablespoon dark sesame oil
¾ cup (60 g) wakame or ito wakame cut into chip-size lengths

In a medium-size skillet over medium heat, warm the sesame oil for about 1 minute.Add the wakame or ito wakame and stir until all the seaweed has been coated with the sesame oil. Turn the heat down to medium low and continue to toast the dried seaweed until crispy, about 2 to 3 minutes.

Serve immediately. Leftovers can be stored in an airtight container in the refrigerator for a few days.

Oven-dried pineapple

This Southeast Asian combination of sweet, salty, spicy and tart flavors makes a great cocktail snack.

Makes about 3 cups (600 g)
2 ripe pineapples, peeled, cored and cut into 1-in (2.5-cm) chunks
¼ cup (60 g) demerara sugar or other raw sugar
2 teaspoons sea salt
1 teaspoon freshly grated nutmeg
2 thai bird chiles, stemmed, deseeded, and finely chopped or ¼ teaspoon ground red pepper (cayenne)
Zest from 2 limes

Preheat the oven to 225°F (105°C). Divide the pineapple chunks between 2 large baking sheets and spread out in a single layer. Bake until the pineapple chunks are golden brown, about 4½ hours. Rotate the pans and flip the pineapple chunks halfway through baking.

Combine the sugar, salt, nutmeg, chiles or ground red pepper and zest in a medium bowl and mix well. When the edges of the pineapple are dried but the center of the fruit is still juicy, remove the baking sheets from the oven and set aside to cool. Toss the pineapple chunks in the spice mixture and transfer to a serving bowl. Serve immediately.

NOTE: If you have a gas oven, you can leave the pineapple in it overnight, turned off; the heat from the pilot light will dry the fruit.

Tamari almonds

Packaged tamari almonds are widely available, but making your own is well worth the effort. A pinch of ground red pepper highlights the tamari flavor without adding heat.

Makes 3 cups (450 g)
3 cups (450 g) whole raw almonds
¼ cup (65 ml) tamari
2 teaspoons sugar
Pinch of ground red pepper (cayenne)

Preheat the oven to 300°F (150°C). Spread the almonds on a sheet pan in an even layer and bake for 15 minutes. Combine the tamari, sugar and cayenne in a glass or metal bowl and mix until the sugar is dissolved. Remove the almonds from the oven and add them to the tamari mixture, tossing to coat. Set aside to marinate for 15 minutes, stirring occasionally. Remove the almonds from the bowl with a slotted spoon and spread them on the sheet pan. Return the pan to the oven and roast the nuts, stirring and turning the pan midway through roasting, until they are dark brown on the outside and golden on the inside, about 20 to 25 minutes. (Cut a nut in half after 20 minutes to check.) Let the almonds cool on the sheet pan, stirring occasionally.

Clockwise from the left: Tamari Almonds, Wakame Chips, Curry Popcorn, Oven-dried Pineapple

Sweet Yam Fries

Sweet yam fries

This is a healthy adaptation of a popular Hong Kong street snack. In this recipe from Monsoon the sweet yams contrast nicely with the Spicy Soy Dipping Sauce. Sambal oelek, a chile-based condiment with a spicy-sweet flavor, can be found in Asian markets and international sections in most grocery stores. For variety, try using a combination of ubiquitous orange yams, sweet potatoes and purple yams.

Serves 4
2 large yams (about 1½ lb/680 g), peeled and cut into ½-in (1.25-cm)-thick batons
2 tablespoons neutral-flavored oil, such as canola
1 teaspoon garlic powder
¼ teaspoon freshly ground black pepper
½ teaspoon salt

SPICY SOY DIPPING SAUCE
¼ cup (60 ml) soy sauce
½ tablespoon sambal oelek

Preheat the oven to 400°F (200°C). Combine the yam batons, oil, garlic powder, black pepper and salt in a large bowl. Mix and toss until the yams are fully coated with the oil and spices. Spread the yams on a baking sheet lined with foil and roast in the oven for 20 minutes or until tender. Once the yams are cooked, remove them from the oven and let them cool for a few minutes.

Combine the soy sauce and sambal oelek in a small bowl and mix well. Serve the yams hot with the Spicy Soy Dipping Sauce.

Curry popcorn

This classic and most simple of bar snacks goes great with cocktails, and it's a great snack to make ahead when entertaining. This Indian-inspired recipe is adapted from www.Rasamalaysia.com.

Makes 2 quarts (110 g)
1 teaspoon cumin seeds
3 tablespoons butter
1 scant tablespoon curry powder
2 tablespoons neutral-flavored oil, such as canola
⅓ cup (75 g) popping corn
Salt

In a small skillet, toast the cumin seeds over medium heat until aromatic, about 30 seconds. Remove the cumin seeds from the skillet and set aside.

In a small saucepan, melt the butter over low heat. Add the curry powder and stir well with a heat-proof rubber spatula, pressing any lumps of curry power until smooth. Bring to a simmer, then set aside.

In a medium saucepan over medium heat, add the oil and the popping corn. Swirl to even coat the popcorn. Cover the pan, leaving the lid slightly open to allow steam to escape (this will create crisper and drier popcorn). Once the popping begins, hold the cover in place and gently shake the pan by moving it back and forth across the burner. When the popping subsides, from the pan from the heat and let rest with the lid still on (but slightly askew) for a few seconds.

Transfer the popcorn to a large bowl. Drizzle on the curry butter while tossing the popcorn to evenly distribute the butter. Sprinkle on the toasted cumin seeds and some salt, if desired, and toss. Serve immediately.

Grilled satays

The popularity of Thai food in the West has created a craze for satay that now extends well beyond Thai restaurants. Many bar and restaurant owners have caught on to the satay trend, offering them up as great bar snacks to accompany drinks or as an appetizer to enjoy with cocktails. The shrimp satay marinade is a delicious fusion of Japanese yakotori, which calls for sake or mirin, and the ingredients in a traditional satay marinade. Satay is truly a worldwide phenomenon! You may serve the satays with one or both of the dipping sauces.

Serves 6 to 8

$\frac{1}{2}$ lb (250 g) pork loin, thinly sliced

3 boneless, skinless chicken thighs, thinly sliced

8 large shrimp, peeled and deveined

30 bamboo skewers, soaked in water for 1 hour before using

2 tablespoons oil, for basting while grilling

Sprigs of fresh coriander leaves (cilantro), for garnish

Pinch of grated lime zest, to garnish shrimp satay

PORK AND CHICKEN MARINADE

2 tablespoons minced garlic

2 tablespoons coarsely chopped fresh coriander stems (cilantro)

1 tablespoon ground coriander

1 teaspoon ground white pepper

2 tablespoons sugar

$\frac{1}{3}$ cup (80 ml) coconut milk (shake before opening)

1 tablespoon fish sauce (nam pla)

SHRIMP MARINADE

$1\frac{1}{2}$ tablespoons fish sauce (nam pla)

3 tablespoons sake

$1\frac{1}{2}$ teaspoons freshly squeezed lemon juice

2 teaspoons Lemongrass Syrup (page 20)

$\frac{1}{2}$ teaspoon finely minced ginger

TANGY DIPPING SAUCE

3 tablespoons fish sauce (nam pla)

3 tablespoons freshly squeezed lime juice

1 tablespoon sugar

1 tablespoon minced fresh red chili pepper or $\frac{1}{4}$ teaspoon crushed red pepper flakes

1 tablespoon thinly sliced garlic

1 tablespoon thinly sliced shallot

1 tablespoon thinly sliced green onion (scallion)

PEANUT DIPPING SAUCE

1 teaspoon neutral-flavored oil

1 clove garlic, minced

1 tablespoon minced shallot

$\frac{1}{4}$ cup (65 ml) coconut milk (shake before opening)

4 tablespoons smooth or crunchy natural peanut butter

1 tablespoon light brown sugar

1 tablespoon freshly squeezed lime juice

1 tablespoon soy sauce

Ground red pepper (cayenne), to taste

In a large bowl, add all of the Pork and Chicken Satay Marinade ingredients. Mix well to combine. Divide the marinade into two resealable plastic bags. Add the pork strips to one bag and the chicken strips to the other. Toss the pork and chicken until well coated and marinate for at least 3 hours or overnight if possible.

Thirty minutes prior to grilling, combine the ingredients for the Shrimp Marinade in a bowl. Add the shrimp and let marinate for 30 minutes.

While the shrimp is marinating, prepare the dipping sauce(s). Combine the ingredients for the Tangy Dipping Sauce, if using, in a small serving bowl. Stir until the sugar is dissolved. Taste and, if needed, dilute with 1 or 2 tablespoons of water. Set aside. To make the Peanut Dipping Sauce, place a small skillet over medium-low heat. Add the oil, garlic and shallot and cook for 1 minute while stirring. Add the remaining ingredients and cook, stirring constantly, for 2 to 3 minutes until well blended. If needed, thin the sauce with additional coconut milk or water.

Preheat a barbecue grill or grill pan to medium or a broiler to low (placing the rack just below the heating element). Brush the hot grill surface or broiler pan with oil just prior to cooking. Thread each marinated pork strip, chicken strip or shrimp onto a presoaked bamboo skewer. Thread all the meat and shrimp in this manner and grill, a few at a time, brushing with a little oil, until nicely seared. The chicken and pork should cook for about 5 minutes on each side, or until cooked through; the shrimp for about 3 minutes on each side, or until opaque. Transfer to a serving platter. Garnish with fresh coriander leaves and lime zest and serve with the Tangy Dipping Sauce and/or the Peanut Dipping Sauce.

Edamame

Edamame, which means "Beans on Branches," is a traditional bar snack in Japan. Slightly nutty and salty, this easy-to-prepare finger food is the perfect accompaniment to enjoying a cocktail. Chef Mitchell Lipperman of Kubu Radio likes to use red volcanic salt to add a touch of color and a flavorful source of trace minerals.

Serves 2 to 3
2¹/₂ cups (300 g) whole frozen or fresh edamame pods
Red volcanic salt, sea salt or kosher salt, to taste

Bring a large pan of water to boil. Add the edamame and boil until just tender, about 3¹/₂ minutes for frozen pods and 5 to 5¹/₂ minutes for fresh pods. Drain the pods well but quickly to maintain the heat and moisture. Toss with the salt and serve immediately. Provide an empty bowl for discarding the pods.

NOTE: Red volcanic salt is also called Hawaiian sea salt, Alaea or Alae sea salt or some combination thereof.

Deviled eggs asian style

Upscale versions of this American favorite have hit the bar snack menus of trendy watering holes. Why not serve up some at home? Japanese mayonnaise is made with rice vinegar, instead of distilled vinegar, which makes it especially complimentary to Japanese cuisine (and Japanese-inspired cocktails!). Japanese mayonnaise can be found at Asian markets or purchased online. Or you can add a little rice vinegar to Western-style mayonnaise to approximate its flavor. Be light-handed with the Japanese red pepper mix. It has a spicy kick that can easily overwhelm the subtle flavor of salmon. The deviled eggs can be made a day ahead if stored well wrapped in the refrigerator.

Makes 8 deviled eggs
4 large eggs
1$\frac{1}{2}$ to 2 tablespoons Japanese mayonnaise, such as the Kewpie brand, or 1$\frac{1}{2}$ to 2 tablespoons Western-style mayonnaise with $\frac{1}{2}$ teaspoon rice vinegar added
$\frac{1}{4}$ teaspoon mirin (sweet rice wine)
Pinch of kosher salt or sea salt
Pinch of white pepper
$\frac{1}{2}$ oz (20 g) smoked salmon, plus extra for garnish
Nori slivers or Japanese red pepper mix (schichimi togarashi), for garnish

Place the eggs and water to cover in a small saucepan and bring to boil over high heat. When the water comes to a boil, remove from the heat and let sit, covered, for 12 minutes. Remove the eggs from the pan and chill thoroughly in ice water for 5 minutes.

Peel the eggs, slice in half lengthwise, and carefully remove the yolks. Place the egg whites on a serving platter. In a small mixing bowl, add the yolks, 1$\frac{1}{2}$ tablespoons of the mayonnaise, the mirin, salt and pepper, and mash until smooth. If you don't feel the mixture is moist enough add another $\frac{1}{2}$ tablespoon of mayonnaise. Flake the salmon over the egg mixture. Stir until thoroughly combined. Spoon the filling back into the whites or, for a fancier presentation, use a pastry bag (or small plastic bag with a snipped corner) to pipe the filling into the whites. Garnish with a small piece of salmon and either nori slivers or a very light dusting of Japanese red pepper mix.

Yuzu lemonade

Yuzu juice adds a certain je ne sais quoi to this classic summer refresher from Pod. For an Asian Shandy, mix equal parts Yuzu Lemonade and Sapporo or your favorite Asian beer.

2 oz (60 ml) Simple Syrup (page 19)
1 oz (30 ml) freshly squeezed lemon juice
$\frac{1}{2}$ oz (15 ml) bottled yuzu juice (unsalted)
Lemon wheel, for garnish
Sprig of mint, for garnish

Combine the ingredients in an iced shaker. Add enough water to fill the shaker and shake vigorously. Pour into a collins glass and add more ice if needed. Garnish with the lemon wheel and sprig of mint.

Yuzu Lemonade

Resources

This guide will help you find most everything you need to make the cocktails in this book. We've included online sources and/or stores that ship for those of you who do not live near Asian markets, gourmet markets or conventional grocery stores with have strong Asian sections. We've included several online stores that sell spirits and wine, however, only about thirty states in America permit shipment of alcoholic beverages. If you live in a state that doesn't permit shipment, simply improvise as best you can, using our suggested substitutions as a guide, or jump in your car and drive to the closet state line. Note that even though bitters contain alcohol, they are classed as a food product and able to be shipped anywhere.

STOCKING YOUR BAR
Brick-and-mortar stores:

Sakaya
324 East 9th Street,
New York, NY 10003,
(212) 505-7253 (SAKE)
www.sakayanyc.com/index.php
Store specializing in sake. They also sell single-pot distilled shochu. They ship.

True Sake
560 Hayes Street,
San Francisco, CA
(415) 355-9555
www.truesake.com/index.php
Store specializing in sake. Nice site for learning about sake. They do not ship.

Sam's Wines & Spirits
Flagship store:1720 N Marcey Street
Chicago (Lincoln Park), IL 60614
(312) 664-4394
www.samswine.com
Store with good selection of spirits, liqueurs, wines, sake and shochu. You can order from their website.

On-line stores:
BevMo!
www.bevmo.com
This is a great one-stop shop for many of the ingredients used in the book from bitters and syrups to liqueurs, wines and spirits.

LOLLICUP USA Inc.
www.lollicupstore.com
Great selection of syrups, including all that are used in this book and many more; some loose teas

Internet Wines & Spirits
www.internetwines.com
They sell much more than wine: shochu, soju, Wokka Saki, Japanese plum wine, sake, Suntory whisky, Zen Green Tea Liqueur.

SakeSocial
www.sakesocial.com
Good source for learning about and purchasing sake.

Bar Supply Warehouse
www.barsupplywarehouse.com/index.html
All types of supplies plus bar kits from the basic home bartending needs to the most professional.

Keg Works
(877) 636-3673
www.kegworks.com
For Luxardo maraschino cherries, cane syrup, orgeat, and a great selection of bitters selection

STOCKING YOUR PANTRY

Agape Tea Company
www.AgapeTea.com
Variety of teas

Asian Food Grocer
www.asianfoodgrocer.com
Sriracha chili sauce, Calpico, canned lychees, Japanese mayonnaise, rice vinegar, mirin, Japanese red pepper mix ("House Red Pepper"), nori, wakame

Earthy Delights
www.earthy.com
Bottled yuzu juice

The Gold Leaf Company
www.goldleafcompany.com/index.html
Edible gold leaf

GourmetSleuth.com
www.gourmetsleuth.com
Bottled yuzu juice

KoaMart
www.koamart.com
Wakame seaweed, jujube tea (They sell a tea with a jellylike consistency rather than the preferred marmalade texture, though it can be used.)

Penzeys Spices
www.penzeys.com
Good selection of all types of spices, including Asian. They also sell vanilla beans and pink peppercorns.

Pinoy Grocery
811 South Mason Road, Suite 116
Katy, Texas 77450
(281) 829-9798
www.store.pinoygrocery.com/index.html;
sales@PinoyGrocery.com
Calamansi products

PilipinoMart
www.pilipinomart.com/index.asp
Calamansi concentrate

Temple of Thai
www.templeofthai.com
Tamarind concentrate, Sriracha chili sauce, dried red dates (jujube), fresh lemongrass and kaffir lime leaves, dried kaffir lime leaves

The Steeping Pot
http://shop.steepingpot.com
Honey granules

Wild Hibiscus
www.wildhibiscus.com
Edible flowers. Bottled hibiscus flowers in syrup ready for use

MISCELLANEOUS RESOURCES

John Gauntner's Sake World
www.sake-world.com
A very good site for information about sake with some information on shochu as well.

Nonjatta
Great reference for learning about Japanese whisky and different types of shochu and how to decipher shochu labeling
http://nonjatta.blogspot.com/
Link to shochu discussion:
http://nonjatta2.blogspot.com/search/label/Basic%20course)

The Shochu
www.maborosi-shochu.com/eng/
Good source of information about shochu

Lenell's
www.lenells.com/index.php
Great site for learning about bitters and a good source of information about interesting and harder-to-find ingredients. As of the publication date of this book the owners are not currently selling and shipping bitters, but they hope to do so in the future—so check their site for updates.

Contributors

Restaurants/Bars

Betty's Wok & Noodle
250 Huntington Avenue, Boston
(617) 424-1950
www.bettyswokandnoodle.com
Pages 83, 84, 87

Buddakan
www.buddakan.com
75 9th Avenue, New York City
212-989-6699
Page 26

325 Chestnut Street, Philadelphia
(215) 574-9440
Pages 50, 88

The Cinnamon Club
The Old Westminster Library
30-32 Great Smith Street, London
020-7222-2555
www.cinnamonclub.com
Pages 28, 53, 58

Jujube
1201-L Raleigh Road, Glen Lennox
Shopping Center, Hwy 54 at 15-501
Chapel Hill, NC
(919) 960-0555
www.jujuberestaurant.com
Pages 51, 66, 70, 72

Kubo Radio
894 Queen Street East,
Toronto (Leslieville)
(416) 406-5826
www.kubo.com
Page 87

Lab Bar
12 Old Compton Street,
London (Soho)
020-7437-7820
www.lab-townhouse.com
Pages 60, 66

Lantern
423 West Franklin Street
Chapel Hill, NC
(919) 969-8846
www.lanternrestaurant.com
Pages 34, 36, 38, 43, 60

Longrain Restaurant & Bar
www.longrain.com.au
Pages 26, 29, 35

Longrain Melbourne
44 Little Bourke Street
Melbourne, Australia
61-3-9671-3151

Longrain Sydney
85 Commonwealth Street
Surry Hills, Sydney, Australia
61-2-9280-2888

Mie N Yu
3125 M Street NW
Washington, D.C.
(202) 333-6122
www.mienyu.com
Pages 26, 37

Miguel Aranda
NYC-based mixologist and consult-
ant. He regularly tends bar at
Apotheke, 9 Doyers Street, NYC
(Chinatown), (212) 406-0400. Miguel
can be contacted via email at
arandabarchef@yahoo.com. He is
part-owner of Speakeasy Cocktail
Consultants (212) 560-2300).
Pages 50, 56, 59, 60, 80, 85

Modus
2202 4th Avenue
San Diego
(619) 236-8516
www.modusbar.com
Pages 31, 41, 77

Monsoon
100 Simcoe Street, Toronto
(416) 979-7172
www.monsoonrestaurant.ca
Pages 31, 62, 91, 103

Morimoto
www.morimotorestaurant.com
88 10th Avenue
New York City
(212) 989-8883
Pages 30, 36

723 Chestnut Street
Philadelphia
215-413-9070
Pages 39, 97

Pod
3636 Sansom Street
Philadelphia
(215) 387-1803
www.podrestaurant.com
Pages 79, 107

Pure Food and Wine
54 Irving Place
New York City
(212) 477-1571
www.purefoodandwine.com
Pages 76, 95

Spring
2039 West North Avenue
Chicago
(773) 395-7100
www.springrestaurant.net
Pages 43, 47, 56, 83

Stanislav Vadrna
www.stanislavvadrna.com
Slovakian-based mixologist, consult-
ant and educator. He is the execu-
tive chef de bar of Red Monkey
Group restaurants/bars, director of
the magazine *Thinking About the
Drinking* and principal of the
Stanislav Vadrnas Analog Bar Insti-
tute. Red Monkey Group has three
restaurants in Bratislava, Slovakia.
Visit www.redmonkeygroup.com for
addresses and telephone numbers.
Pages 66, 79, 88

Starry Night Café
5371 Rt. 7
Ferrisburg, VT
(802) 877-6316
www.starrynightcafe.com
Pages 42, 48, 62

SushiSamba
Locations in NYC, Chicago, Miami,
Las Vegas and Telaviv
Visit www.sushisamba.com for ad-
dresses and telephone numbers
Page 40

Others

Bee Yinn Low
Rasa Malaysia: Asian Cooking &
Recipes
www.rasamalaysia.com
Page 103

Saveur
www.saveur.com
Recipe first published as "Oven-
Dried Spicy Pineapple Snacks" in
Saveur, issue no. 96
Page 100 (right)

**Taekyung Chung and Debra
Samuels**
Co-authors of *The Korean Table*
www.cookingatdebras.com
Page 100

contributors

Index

asian cocktails

acknowledgments

Christine and I would like to thank all of the mixologists and chefs from around the world who contributed cocktails and bar snacks to this book. I'd also like to thank Yukari Sakamoto for answering my questions about shochu (http://tokyostation-yukari.blogspot.com/). I am indebted to Gary Regan for teaching me the basics of making a good drink, to my friend Todd for accompanying me on our cocktail "workshops" at Milk and Honey in NYC, and to Mike for putting up with sticky counters during endless testing rounds. Gorta would like to thank the following people and businesses for helping to facilitate the photography for the book:

Ms. Kikuko Fujimoto and Ms. Yoko Fujimoto (for making the cocktails)

Chinatsu Kambayashi (for styling)

Zwiesel Boutique (for supplying glassware)
FLEG Daikanyama 1F
1-31-12 Ebisu-Nishi Shibuya-Ku
Tokyo 150-0021 Japan
Tel: +81-3-3770-3553
www.zwiesel-kristallglas.jp

Gallup East Showroom (for supplying backgrounds and props)
1F 2-4-4 Tomioka Kouto-Ku
Tokyo 135-0047 Japan
Tel: +81-3-5639-9633
www.thegallup.com

House Restaurant (for providing on-site settings)
Show Case 4F
2-24-7 Nishiazabu Minato-Ku
Tokyo 106-0031 Japan
Tel: +81-3-6418-1595

bills SHICHIRIGAHAMA café/restaurant (for providing on-site settings)
WEEKEND HOUSE ALLEY 2F
Shichirigahama Kamakura-Shi
Kanagawa-Ken 248-0026 Japan
www.bills-jp.net